THE GOOD,
THE BAD
AND THE
RIDICULOUS

THE **GOOD,**
THE **BAD**
AND THE
RIDICULOUS

~ profiles ~

**KHUSHWANT
SINGH**

with Humra Quraishi

RUPA

Published by
Rupa Publications India Pvt. Ltd 2013
7/16, Ansari Road, Daryaganj
New Delhi 110002

Sales centres:
Allahabad Bengaluru Chennai
Hyderabad Jaipur Kathmandu
Kolkata Mumbai

ISBN: 978-81-291-2443-2

10 9 8 7 6 5 4 3 2 1

The moral right of the author has been asserted.

Typeset by Jojy Philip, New Delhi.

Printed at Thomson Press India Ltd, Faridabad.

CONTENTS

INTRODUCTION

I have never been a very tactful person. I have never been discreet either. I am a voyeur and a gossip. I am also very opinionated. These are good qualities to have if your aim is to be a writer who is read. You could add to that the extremely useful habit of keeping a diary.

I have met a good number of this subcontinent's most famous (or infamous) and interesting people. I have also suffered famous bores, and sometimes been rewarded with behaviour so ridiculous that it becomes compelling. One reason why I have found myself around so many well-known people is that I was in professions which made this possible:

journalism, law and public relations for India's foreign missions. Another reason is that my father was a successful contractor and builder and he sent me to schools and colleges where the children of the rich and famous of the day studied. Several of them later became rich and famous themselves.

Through the latter half of my life, I have had the luxury of having some of the high and mighty of India, Pakistan and other neighbouring countries come to me. I have never understood why. It is true that I live in a comfortable flat in one of Delhi's more pleasant areas, and I am generous with my Scotch. But I also insist that nobody should ring my doorbell unless they are expected, and certainly not before 7 p.m., and then I ask everyone to finish their drinks and bugger off before 8 p.m. Besides, I get easily bored and now, at death's door, very easily tired. Still, people keep coming to spend time with me. Maybe they have nothing better to do. Or maybe they are being kind to an old man and want to keep him company—even if he would be happier without it.

I have seen prominent people at close quarters or been privy to facts about them that are not widely known. A lot of what I have observed or found out is not flattering, but I have never held back from making all of it public in my columns and books. If what is good in a person can be written about, why not the bad? I don't do this out of malice, only out of my firm belief in being truthful. I cannot cheat myself or my readers. If I am proved wrong, I will gladly admit my mistake.

I have been criticized most severely for writing uncomplimentary things about dead people. No one seems to disagree with me that the person concerned was a windbag or a liar or a brute. Their objection is that I do not respect the dead. I find this hypocritical. Death does not wipe away the sins of nastiness or idiocy. A man should be judged in death as he would be in life. The truly good and the great are not diminished when their faults are exposed; on the contrary, they earn greater respect for rising to admirable heights despite their very human flaws.

I have no fear of people being nasty to me in print. If I cannot ignore the criticism or venom, I join in the laughter. I wish everyone would do that. Instead, some of them get very angry. And when they cannot do you physical harm or prove you wrong by fair means, they take you to court for libel or worse. I should know. I had this done to me by Maneka Gandhi. She did not like the little that she read of my autobiography in a pre-publication excerpt in *India Today*. She went to court and got a stay on publication. Nothing that I had written was a lie, but it was her word against mine, and I was up against a legal system run by thin-skinned and humourless humbugs. I had to wait some years before my autobiography could be published, and only after some lines were deleted.

I don't wish to be dragged to court again. Death threats don't scare me, but I fear court cases that can go on for decades. There is enough in this book to inform, entertain and perhaps shock the reader. But, alas, I cannot name the large lady politician who told me of her passion for Rajiv Gandhi and hatred of Sonia for having cheated her of Rajiv's love. Nor can I name the overrated poetess who seduced a legendary Urdu poet and songwriter only to find that he could not get it up. I cannot write about the Indian president who pulled out a bottle of premium whisky from under his bed and shared a drink with me. I cannot tell you what I have heard about a central minister's love of al fresco sex, or a right-wing leader's dealings with an underworld don.

To read all these stories and more, you will have to wait till I am dead and a suicidal publisher decides to print them. For now, enjoy this book of profiles of the good, bad and ridiculous people I have known over almost a century.

ALI SARDAR JAFRI

(1913–2000)

The day Ali Sardar Jafri died in Bombay (1 August 2000, at 8.30 a.m.)—an ironic death in a season of troubled détente—I made it a point to watch Pakistan Television to find out what it had to say about him. Jafri was not only in the front rank of Urdu poets in recent times but also the spearhead of the movement for rapproachement with Pakistan. PTV made a passing reference to Jafri's death as a poet who wrote of the need for love and understanding between people. I was disappointed. I was also disappointed by the coverage given by the Indian media, both print and electronic. There was more to Jafri than the hastily written obituaries and collages put together to meet deadlines.

I had known Ali Sardar Jafri and his beautiful wife, Sultana, for over thirty years and, during my years in Bombay, we met each other almost every other week. Despite his commitment to communism, Ali Sardar liked the good things in life: good Scotch, good food and comfortable living. He lived in a pokey little three-room flat off Peddar Road. Apart from his wife and three children, who often stayed with him, he had two widowed sisters living in the same apartment. There was not much room to move about and many of his books were stacked under his bed, upon which he read, wrote and slept.

I would arrive armed with a bottle of Scotch; then Ali Sardar would send for soda and biryani from a restaurant, Allah Beli, facing his apartment. I sought out his company because he was one of the most erudite Indian writers I had met. He also had a phenomenal memory. If I quoted a line by any Urdu poet, he would come out with the rest of the poem. And explain every word by referring to Persian poets—from Rumi and Hafiz to Ghalib and Allama Iqbal.

When I set about translating Iqbal's 'Shikwa' and 'Jawab-e-Shikwa', I travelled all the way to Bombay to seek Ali Sardar's assistance. For two days, he and Sultana came to my hotel in the morning; we worked till lunchtime, when Rafiq Zakaria and his wife, Fatma, joined us to find out how it was going. After they left, we resumed our labours till it was time for our sundowners.

I often needled Ali Sardar about his communism. He had been a cardholder and had been expelled from the Aligarh Muslim University (which later gave him an honorary doctorate) and spent eighteen months in jail during the British Raj, and again after independence, under Morarji Desai's government. Although he had ceased to be a cardholder, he stoutly defended Marxist ideology. What was beyond my comprehension was that despite professing atheism, during the month of Muharram, he often wore black and attended Shia majlis and abstained from alcohol. During a television interview with me, wherein he expected to be questioned about Urdu poetry, I confronted him with his contradictory beliefs in both Islam and Marxism. He was visibly upset and fumbled for words, then took it out on me after the interview

was over. He called me everything under the sun,
stopping just short of calling me a bastard. Had he
not been so obsessed with communism and social
problems, I am convinced he would have been a
greater poet.

Ali Sardar was also an incorrigible optimist.
Inspired by Rumi's line 'Hum cho sabza baarha
roeeda aym'—like the green of the earth, we never
stop growing—Ali Sardar summed up his life story,
'Mera Safar', thus in a few memorable lines:

> I am a fleeting moment
> In the magic house of days and nights;
> I am a restless drop travelling eternally
> From the flask of the past to the goblet of the
> future.
> I sleep and wake, awake to sleep again;
> I am the ancient play on the stage of time—
> I die only to become immortal.

AMRITA SHER-GIL

(1913-1941)

Women seduce. That is a fact. I have been seduced by women all my life, right from the time I was attracted to my first love, Ghayoor—it was she who had held my hand. Most women have made the first pass at me, led me on, with the exception of two women, wherein I took the lead. Even when I was attracted to a woman, I had little confidence to make the first move; instead, I was terribly flattered when women made a pass at me. Looking back, I wish I had the confidence to make the first move, for I could have got closer to several women, like the now legendary painter Amrita Sher-Gil. Amrita, you see, had threatened to seduce me. It happened in Shimla in the mid-1930s.

Amrita came into my sitting room (and my life) one day and introduced herself. She told me of the flat she had rented across the road, and wanted advice about carpenters, plumbers, tailors and the like. I tried to size her up. I couldn't look her in the face too long because she had that bold, brazen kind of look that makes timid men like me turn their gaze down.

She was short and sallow-complexioned (being half Sikh and half Hungarian). Her hair was parted in the middle and tightly bound at the back. She had a bulbous nose, with black heads showing. She had thick lips with a faint shadow of a moustache. Politeness, I discovered, was not one of her virtues; she believed in speaking her mind, however rude or unkind it be.

As a baby, my son, Rahul, was in the playpen, learning to stand on his feet. Everyone was paying him compliments: he was a very pretty little child with curly hair, large, questioning eyes and dimpled cheeks. 'What an ugly little boy!' remarked Amrita. Others protested their embarrassment. My wife froze. Amrita continued to drink her beer without concern.

Later, when she heard what my wife had to say about her manners, that she had described her as a 'bloody bitch', Amrita told her informant: 'I will teach that woman a lesson. I will seduce her husband.'

There were stories that Amrita had seduced many well-known characters of that time. People like the art critic Karl Khandalawala, Iqbal Singh and her nephew, the painter Vivan Sundaram, have written books on Amrita; Badruddin Tyebji has given a vivid account of how he was seduced by her—she simply took off her clothes and lay herself naked on the carpet by the fireplace. Vivan admits to her having many lovers; according to him, her real passion in life was another woman.

Unfortunately, Amrita couldn't carry out her threat of seducing me because she died a few months later. She was not yet thirty then.

BALWANT GARGI

(1916–2003)

I will never understand why Balwant Gargi committed adultery and then sat and wrote about it.

I don't recall when I first met Gargi, except that it was at the home of a good-looking lass whom he had succeeded in leading astray from the straight and narrow path of matrimony. What had she found in him? He was a short, squat man who punctuated his talk with effeminate gestures and walked with a mincing gait, like one afraid of slipping.

Gargi was said to be a good playwright; but since he wrote in Punjabi and only rarely were his plays staged, few people knew his real worth. I did not read or watch any of his plays, but I did get to read an anthology of profiles: they were the wittiest pieces of prose I had ever read in Punjabi. They were obviously designed to hurt, and succeeded in doing so. Thereafter, every time Gargi produced a book, he lost a dozen of his close friends. He made up for the loss by acquiring new admirers. He was certainly an engaging talker and had the knack of surrounding himself with attractive women, successfully persuading quite a few of them that a Dunlopillo mattress was not what was necessary to make the bed an exciting place.

In his younger days, Gagi professed communism (we all did), then jettisoned it (so did we) and landed a job to teach Indian theatre at Seattle University. He produced an excellent book on Indian theatre in English; I complimented him on writing 300 pages on a subject that did not exist. He returned from Seattle with a lovely blonde American wife, Jeannie, and all of his friends fell in love with her. It was a misalliance. Gargi's diet was literary sarson ka saag; Jeannie was American apple pie. Gargi wanted appreciation for what he wrote; Jeannie never bothered to learn Punjabi and was therefore unable to become a part of her husband's claque. Gargi was gregarious, open-hearted in his hospitality, with not much in his kitty to be open-hearted about; Jeannie cherished the privacy of her home and could not stomach people dropping in at all hours. She also had an enormous appetite for food, which embarrassed Gargi for the simple reason that his friends might think he did not give her enough to eat at home. It was Gargi who took the irrevocable step to break up the marriage by committing adultery.

Gargi wrote an emotionally charged account of his lustful encounter with one of his girl students in a garage, through the window of which could see his wife and children. It was a detailed and lusty account of the love-making, describing even the size of her breasts and her nipples. And that was the end of his marriage with the beautiful Jeannie.

In his semi-autobiographical novel *The Naked Triangle*, Gargi barely concealed the identity of the people he wrote about, and some were mentioned by their real names. There was the writer and film producer Rajinder Singh Bedi, recounting his affair with a nineteen-year-old girl who bared her bosom to him as a sort of introductory 'how do you do?'—it made for nice erotica, but it does not need much imagination to know how the lady in the episode, Mrs Bedi, her children and grandchildren would react to this disclosure. The book was largely set in Chandigarh, and Punjab University's academic circle was up in arms against him for having portrayed them with their shirts up, pants and shalwars down. Balwant Gargi was like a cactus—he hurt anyone he touched.

After his marriage ended, Gargi was a heartbroken man and lived in New Delhi under financial strain before shifting with his son to Bombay. In his later years, I was told, he was struck by Alzheimer's disease.

BEGUM PARA

(1926–2008)

In the early 1970s, I visited Pakistan twice to see how Zulfiqar Ali Bhutto was doing, and how Pakistan was taking the drubbing of its army by the Indian forces in the 1971 war. The second of these visits turned out more interesting, as among the people I met was Begum Para. That meeting has remained one of my most memorable encounters.

I had first met Begum Para through Rukhsana Sultana, who was her niece and married to my nephew. One-time super-vamp of the Indian screen, Begum Para had put on a lot of weight after she married Nasir Khan (brother of superstar Yusuf

Khan, a.k.a, Dilip Kumar). She had borne him two lovely children—a daughter and a son—and I had met them several times in Bombay when she was living there. Many a Sunday morning, the family would join me at the Gymkhana Club bathing pool to swim and have breakfast.

When Nasir died, he left behind very little besides a flat in Bandra and a couple of films. Now, Begum Para felt that she had a right to some of the millions that her brother-in-law was making; however, this was to no avail. So she frequently brought up the question of money: if anyone could loan her forty or fifty thousand rupees, she would say, she could have her old films rescreened and make a fortune. I didn't take the hint.

In sheer desperation, Begum Para eventually abandoned Bombay for Pakistan, where she had a considerable inheritance waiting to be claimed. But it didn't take her long to discover that her relatives were not willing to part with anything, and she was on weak ground, having earlier opted for India. She earned a little by flogging films she had brought with her and appearing on television. Her children too were unhappy; after the free and easy atmosphere of Bombay, the girl, who was

rapidly growing into a beautiful young lady, found
the puritanical atmosphere of Pakistan particularly
stifling. They wanted rather badly to return to
Bombay.

Begum Para had written me several letters, asking
for help in returning to India; I wrote back that I
would be visiting Karachi soon and we could talk
the matter over.

When I arrived in Karachi early in the evening,
Begum Para and her children were at the airport to
receive me. So was the chief of protocol, as I was
a guest of the government. We were conducted to
the VIP lounge, where the children had their fill
of cakes and biscuits. Once they were sent home,
Begum Para accepted my invitation to dine with me
at the hotel where I was to stay the night. The chief
of protocol dropped us at my hotel, and Begum
Para accompanied me to my room.

I ordered soda and ice and took out the bottle
of Scotch I had brought with me. There was, at
that time, no prohibition in Pakistan. I had heard
stories about Begum Para's drink problem; she had
apparently been forced to cut down on it because of
the price: a bottle of Scotch cost twice as much in
Pakistan as it did in India.

'Would you like a drink?' I asked her, unsure whether she was still a drinking woman.

'I'll take a little,' she replied. 'I haven't seen genuine Scotch for ages.'

I poured out two stiff whiskies and handed her one. I was not even halfway through my glass when I saw that hers was empty. I poured her another one, which she tossed back instantly; I had to refill her glass once more before I resumed my own drinking.

By the time I had finished my quota of three large whiskies, Begum Para had had nine and the bottle was almost empty. I told her then that we must eat soon as I had to catch the early-morning flight to Islamabad. Reluctantly, she got up to go with me to the dining room.

The dining room was on the first floor and we had to climb up a spiral marble staircase to get to it. The place was crowded, but, as was usual in Pakistan, there were very few women there. People recognized Begum Para because of her appearances on television. It was quite evident that they were intrigued to see her in the company of a Sikh. She had another two whiskies before the soup was served. She had begun to slur over her words and

her eyes had taken on a glazed look. She wanted to
have yet another drink with her meal, but I put my
foot down.

At long last, the meal came to an end and I got
up to assist Begum Para with her chair. She stood
up, swayed a little and collapsed on the carpet.
The waiters came running to help her get back to
her feet. I took her arm to help her walk to the
stairs. All eyes in the dining room had turned to
us, and I was doubly careful going down the spiral
staircase. I gripped her fat arm. 'One step at a time,'
I instructed her. We finally made it to the foyer. I
ordered a taxi for her and waited patiently for the
ordeal to be over.

A taxi drew up in the portico. I gave the driver a
hundred-rupee note and told him to take the lady
home. He recognized Begum Para and knew where
she lived. I opened the rear door of the taxi and
went back to help her. As she stepped forward, she
missed her step and, once again, collapsed on the
ground, this time with a loud fart. She had sprained
her ankle and began to howl in pain: 'Hai rabba,
main mar gayee!'—Oh God, I'm dead!

A crowd had gathered, but no one came forward
to help. Being an Islamic country, no unrelated

male could touch a woman. I did my best to haul Begum Para up to her feet by myself. She was far too heavy for me. I pleaded with the taxi driver for help. My advance tip came in handy—he acquiesced. Together, we got Begum Para on her feet and pushed her into the seat. I slammed the door shut and bid her a hurried farewell, swearing to forever steer clear of divas given to drink.

That was my last encounter with Begum Para. But when I heard of her passing in 2008, I was deeply saddened, remembering only the pleasure of those shared Sunday breakfasts long ago in Bombay.

BHAGAT PURAN SINGH
(1904–1992)

Sometime in 1980, I happened to be addressing a convocation of the Khalsa College in Amritsar. I noticed an old man with a scraggy long beard, an untidy white turban wrapped around his head, dressed in khadi kurta-pyjama, engrossed in taking notes on what I was saying. I could not take my eyes off him. He disappeared as soon as the convocation was over. Later, I asked the principal of the college, who was sharing the dais with me, about the old man in the front row. 'You don't know him?' he asked in surprise. 'That was Bhagat Singh of the Pingalwara.'

'What was he writing while the speeches were going on?' I asked.

'He always does that,' replied the principal. 'If he hears anything worthwhile, he puts it in his newspaper published in Punjabi and English. In the Pingalwara, he has his own printing press.'

Bhagat Puran Singh had become a household name long before I saw him. On a subsequent visit to Amritsar, I noticed small, black tin boxes, with the word Pingalwara written in white on them, in different parts of the city. These had a slit on top, through which people could put in money. I learnt that Bhagat Puran Singh was to be seen on the steps of the Golden Temple as well, holding out the hem of his kurta for people to drop alms for his home for destitutes. It had also become a practice in many families to send money to the Pingalwara when there was a wedding in the house or in memory of a deceased family member. Neither the Punjab government nor the municipality gave him any financial assistance; it was only the people who gave him just enough to feed, clothe and render medical assistance to over 800 sick men, women and children abandoned by their families.

I was intrigued and determined to meet him.

From Delhi I wrote to him seeking an appointment to visit the Pingalwara and talk to him. I got a reply in Gurmukhi, written in his own hand, asking me to come as soon as I could. Three days later, I was back in Amritsar. I took a taxi from the railway station and arrived at the Pingalwara.

The first thing Bhagatji asked me was: 'How did you come here?'

'By train from Delhi, then by cab from the station,' I replied, somewhat bewildered by the question. Maybe he thought I had flown in.

'You should have come by tonga or on a bicycle,' he said quite firmly.

'Where would I find a bicycle on hire at the railways station? And a tonga would have taken more than an hour to get here,' I protested.

Bhagatji gave me a dressing down: 'Do you know how much poisonous gas a motor car emits and fouls the air?' He then proceeded to give me a long lecture on global warming and what it would do to human and animal life, forests and vegetation. He thrust some sheets of his newsletter in my hand, commanding me: 'Read this, and this, and this.'

Clearly, he was somewhat of a crackpot. I love crackpots.

I went round the Pingalwara. It did not answer the requirements of modern hygiene. People were lying on charpoys with flies buzzing around. Lavatory stench, mixed with the smell of phenyl and food being cooked, pervaded the air. Volunteers scurried around, doing the best they could. It was evident that there was shortage of everything—food, clothes, medicines, staff. How much could one man do to help 800 people?

I made a nominal donation, gathered all the printed material Bhagatji gave me and retuned to Delhi.

Back home, I wrote in my columns about Bhagatji's dedicated service and the odds he was facing. I wrote to the Punjab chief minister and whomever else I could think of. The response was heartening. More money began to flow into the Pingalwara.

Thereafter, whenever Bhagatji came to Delhi, he dropped in to see me. I did not chide him for coming in a taxi but made a token offering, which he accepted without counting the notes. A receipt followed some days later.

Bhagatji's work began to receive wider recognition. People began to make donations on a regular basis. Conditions in the Pingalwara improved and its activities expanded. No discrimination was ever made on grounds of religion or caste: the inmates included Hindus, Sikhs and Muslims; there were Brahmins, Kshatriyas, Vaishyas, Shudras and Harijans. Suffering knows no caste.

The last time I met Bhagatji was a few weeks after Operation Blue Star, which had taken a heavy toll of lives and caused extensive damage to sacred property. My reaction was immediate. Within twenty-four hours of the army assault on the Golden Temple, I had returned my Padma Bhushan to President Giani Zail Singh as a mark of protest. Bhagatji asked me if he should do the same with the Padma Shri he had been awarded in 1979; a week later, he relinquished the honour bestowed on him.

When Bhagatji died, I paid a tearful tribute to him in my columns. A few years later, I persuaded my brothers and sister to make a substantial donation on behalf of the Sir Shobha Singh Charitable Trust to the Pingalwara. It was graciously accepted by Dr Inderjit Kaur, who had taken over its management. Some months later, Dr Manmohan Singh, then minister of finance, accompanied our family to Amritsar to inaugurate a new block for patients in the Pingalwara.

It was impossible to meet Bhagatji and not feel inspired to contribute towards his mission in some manner, however modest—and his legacy of dedicated service to suffering humanity must be kept alive for generations to come. In living memory, Punjab has not produced as great a man as Bhagat Puran Singh.

CHETAN ANAND

(1921-1997)

During the years I spent at Government College, Lahore, in the early 1930s, I got to know a lot of people who later made it to the top—or near the top—in the film industry. Two years senior to me was Balraj Sahni; his younger brother Bhisham, B.R. Chopra and Chetan Anand were in the same class as me. Of them, closest to me was Chetan, who was quite a character.

Chetan was a pretty boy with curly hair and soulful eyes. He was much sought after by tough lads who fancied effeminate males; Chetan avoided them like the plague and attached himself to me. We walked from our hostel to the college together, sat side by side in our classes, played tennis and went to the pictures. Although tongues wagged, there was nothing homosexual about our relationship. Like me, Chetan too aspired to get into the ICS and came to England to sit for the exams. Neither of us made the grade. I returned to Lahore with a law degree; he had no more than the BA he had taken from Punjab University. Desperately looking for a job, Chetan spent a summer at my apartment. It was then that I saw another side to him.

Women found Chetan very attractive, and he had a unique method of ingratiating himself with them. On the hottest days in June, he would go out wearing his overcoat; with a stubble on his chin and a single flower in his hand, he would call on his lady friends. Inevitably, the dialogue would open with the young lady asking him why he was wearing an overcoat. 'This is all I possess in the world,' Chetan would reply as he presented her with the flower. He had phenomenal success with this approach.

In due course, Chetan succeeded in winning the heart of the most sought-after girl at the university, Uma Chatterji—though she was a Christian, she defied her parents and agreed to marry a Hindu boy who had no job. I threw a large party to celebrate their engagement, and discovered the fickleness in Chetan's character: he flirted outrageously with all the other girls at the party! The next morning, when I reprimanded him and called him a 'haraami', he smiled disarmingly and brushed away my protests. Chetan and Uma were married and had two children. But Uma could not take his philandering after a point and left him; she later married the producer and arts collector Ebrahim Alkazi. Chetan, in the meantime, shacked up with a Sikh girl young enough to be his daughter.

Chetan and I kept in touch over the years. I wrote to him about his films (he only made one good one), and he produced the son-et-lumière programmes at the Red Fort in Delhi, based on a script written by me. I heard from others that he had claimed to have written the text as well, but when I questioned him he denied ever having made such a claim. Later, of course, there were others who made similar claims.

When I moved to Bombay to take up the editorship of *The Illustrated Weekly of India* in the late 1960s, I was eager to renew my acquaintance with friends from my Lahore days, who had by now become big names in the film world. Most of all, I was looking forward to reconnecting with Chetan, since he had enjoyed my hospitality on innumerable occasions and had been one of my closest friends. I spent many weekends at Balraj Sahni's villa in Juhu; B.R. Chopra asked me to his home a couple of times, as did Kamini Kaushal; once a week, I dined with I.S. Johar and his ex-wife, Rama Bans; even Dev Anand invited me to his large cocktail parties. But Chetan Anand, whom I had expected to see more than anyone else, remained mysteriously unwelcoming. He only rang me up a few times, when he wanted publicity for something he was doing. Usually, he ended the dialogue with a vague 'Kabhi humare ghar aana.' I was very disappointed and angry.

A few months before I was due to leave Bombay, I ran into Chetan and his lady friend at a party. 'Why haven't you come to our home? ' she asked.

I exploded: 'Because I have never been asked by that kameena friend of yours!'

People can be divided into givers and takers, suckers and spongers—Chetan Anand was the biggest taker and sponger I have met in my life.

DHIRENDRA BRAHMACHARI

(1924-1994)

I first met Dhirendra Brahmachari when he had recently installed himself in Delhi as teacher of 'hatha yoga' and was eager to cultivate people in high positions. A senior official from the ministry of education (he was seeking a grant from the ministry for his ashram) brought him to my apartment, and he instructed me on the appropriate asanas for the imaginary ailments from which I have always suffered.

I was very taken with Dhirendra Brahmachari's unusually handsome appearance: tall, ramrod-straight, with the cleanest and clearest eyes I had ever seen. His gossamer-thin dhoti worn on the coldest day of the year could not fail to impress anyone about his physical fitness—he was the living example of what he taught and practised. He had more charisma than any other yogi, sadhu or swami I had met.

We struck up a passing acquaintance and I met him on several occasions. He even sent me the manuscript of his book *Yogasanas* for corrections. I spent a New Year's morning at his ashram to interview him and his patients for an article for the *New York Times*. By then, he had become a prosperous and powerful man. Despite being a semi-literate yoga instructor from Bihar, Dhirendra Brahmachari had managed to acquire considerable influence with Indira Gandhi and was one of her advisors and confidantes on domestic affairs. He had his own aircraft, imported cars, a herd of Jersey cows, a gun factory and other real estate. He was even cited as a co-respondent in a divorce case.

To be fair to him, though, Dhirendra Brahmachari did not exploit his chelas, only the people who exploited him to forward their own interests. However, it was clear as daylight that he had his feet in two different boats, the spiritual and the material, and would inevitably come to grief. I believe that it was this ambivalence in his character—the desire to get the best of both the worlds—that roused people's ire and jealousy. They rejoiced when he was taken off television and chortled with pleasure when they read of the seizure of his gun factory. Many of us felt that his fortune was undeserved.

My *New York Times* piece on sadhus was a rather critical one. Soon after it was published, Dhirendra Brahmachari called me and said, 'Aapne kuchh aisa likha hai, ki chott lagai hai'—you have written something that has hurt me. But I did not give a damn, for his stuff was all humbug.

DOM MORAES

(1938–2004)

Dom Moraes's interest in poetry was born very early in his life. In his preface to a collection of his poems, he wrote, 'I was about ten years old when I started to read poetry... I had an instinctive feel, even at that age, for the shape and texture of words.' By the time he was fourteen, Dom—Domsky to his friends—had begun to write poetry himself, and he learnt French in order to be able to read Villon in the original. Poetry became a lifelong passion and he continued to write till the end of his life.

Dom was my friend from his years at Jesus College, Oxford. He was a complex character who disliked everything about India, particularly Indians—the only exceptions he made were the good-looking women he took to bed. Although he was born in Bombay and dark as a Goan, Dom considered himself English, spoke no Indian language and wished to be buried in the churchyard of Odcombe, a tiny village in Somerset. Never a practising Christian, he selected Odcombe because one Thomas Coryate, who hailed from the village, had travelled all the way from England to India in the seventeenth century and died in Surat, where he is buried—and Dom went to Odcombe with Sarayu Srivatsa, his companion during the last decade and a half of his life, to collect material on Coryate's background for his biography. Despite his distaste for India, however, Dom's descriptions of the Indian countryside—of the heat and dust storms of summer, of the monsoons—were lyrically beautiful. His characters too came alive in his writing; notwithstanding his ignorance of the Indian languages, Dom was able to comprehend what people said in their dialects and in Indian-English.

Like his father, Frank Moraes, Dom was a heavy drinker. Because of his love for the bottle, Dom could not be depended on for meeting deadlines or sticking to the subject he was commissioned to write on. Ram Nath Goenka of *The Indian Express* sacked Dom for spending his time in a Calcutta hotel, drinking and consorting with a lady, instead of going on his assignment to the Northeast. His friend R.V. Pandit fired him for drinking in his office in Hong Kong. *The Times of India* appointed him editor of a magazine they intended to bring out, but they fired him before the first issue came out; Dom vented his anger on poor Prem Shankar Jha, who was appointed in his stead, by grabbing his tie and demanding: 'Fatty boy! What do you know about journalism?'

I had got Dom an assignment from the Dempos, shipping magnates and mine-owners of Goa; Dom produced a very readable book on Goa without mentioning the Dempos—I had to add four pages on the family. He was commissioned by the Madhya Pradesh tourism department to do a book on the state's historical sites; he did a creditable job of describing the beauty of the landscape and the state's full-bosomed tribal women, without bothering about historical sites. Dom never allowed facts or truths to stand in the way of his writing. He did not write reference books; instead, he painted pictures in vivid colours to the songs of flutes.

Dom is said to have married thrice. When he was married to the actress Leela Naidu, I stayed with them in Hong Kong; they, in turn, visited me several times in Delhi. At the best of times, Dom spoke in a low mumble, hard to understand—when I had asked Indira Gandhi, whom he interviewed many times to write her biography, if she understood what he said, she had beamed and replied, 'No, Leela Naidu translated for me.' Dom's second wife, Judy, bore him a son, although I don't think Dom paid for his education; neither am I sure if he had church or civil weddings and court divorces. In any event, he certainly did not pay any alimony to his former wives—he never earned enough to do so.

Dom was not choosy about his women: if any of them were willing, he was always ready to oblige. The only real love of his life, I think, was Sarayu, a Tamilian Brahmin married to a Punjabi and the mother of two children.

Sarayu was instrumental in Dom's overcoming of the writers' block that plagued him for seventeen long years, from 1965 to 1982. In partnership with her, Dom wrote *Out of God's Oven*, perhaps the most fascinating example of his condemnation of all things Indian that he hated. Between them, Dom and Sarayu traversed the length and breadth of India, interviewing poets, writers, editors, film producers, Naxalites, Ranbir Sena leaders, dacoits and politicians—and Dom decried the resurgence of Hindu fundamentalism in the Bajrang Dal, the Shiv Sena, the Hindu Vishwa Parishad, the Bharatiya Janata Party and its progenitor, the Rashtriya Swayamsevak Sangh, exposing their vandalism, their penchant for violence and their pathological hatred of Muslims.

While his prose was limpid and lyrical, Dom's verse was not easy to read. His words had resonance, but one had to read every line two or three times before one could comprehend its meaning—people brought up on simple rhyming verse such as 'Twinkle, twinkle, little star' would likely find Dom's poems difficult. One could, however, detect a few themes that recurred consistently in his poems: he was obsessed with death; the hawk was the symbol of doom; his mother's insanity haunted him all his life; and he sought escape in hard liquor and making love. He summed it up in 'A Letter':

My father hugging me so hard it hurt,
My mother mad, and time we went away.
We travelled, and I looked for love too young.
More travel, and I looked for lust instead.
I was not ruled by wanting: I was young,
And poems grew like maggots in my head.

With Sarayu's arrival, Dom turned to writing about love. In poetry he said of her:

Fourteen years, the same mixture
As when first I met her:
... Her breasts always ready:
Mindmarks and handmarks on each other:
I study the landscape of her body
As architect, husband, and brother.

... We have been more than married. It was
meant.
We've lived in each other. It was meant to be.

When Dom was stricken with cancer, he refused to undergo chemotherapy. It was as if he almost wallowed in the prospect of an early end, with the ghost of his insane mother hovering over him.

From a heavenly asylum, shrivelled Mummy,
glare down like a gargoyle at your only son.
... That I'm terminally ill hasn't been much
    help.
There is no reason left for anything to exist.
Goodbye now. Don't try to meddle with this.

Dom Moraes died in his sleep on the evening of Wednesday, 2 June 2004, and was buried in the Sewri Christian Cemetery in Bombay. He was only sixty-eight. With him died the best of Indian poets of the English language, and the greatest writer of felicitous prose.

FAIZ AHMAD FAIZ

(1911-1984)

Faiz Ahmad Faiz was two years my senior in college—and exactly five years older, to the day, than my wife. He was studying for masters' degrees in English and Arabic in Lahore and, though a student, had already been admitted to the charmed circle of Lahore's Aesthetics Club, comprising Professor A.S. Bokhari (Patras), Imtiaz Ali Taj, Muhammad Din Taseer and Sufi Tabassum. This was due to his reputation as an up-and-coming poet.

Faiz had been composing poetry ever since he was sixteen. At his first public appearance at a mushaira in Murray College, Sialkot (from where he had taken a bachelor's degree), he had made his mark with a couplet:

Lab bund hain saaqi, meree aakhin ko pilaa
Voh jaam jo minnatkash-e-sehba nahin hota

My lips are sealed, saaqi let these eyes of mine
   take a sip
Without drawing to ask for wine

A few years later, when I returned from England and made my home in Lahore, Faiz and I resumed our acquaintance. Following the instructions of the Communist Party of India, Faiz had joined the British Army and wore an officer's uniform. It was about this time that Alys, whose elder sister was married to Taseer, came to India to marry Harkirat Singh (later a general) to whom she was engaged while he was a cadet at Sandhurst. By then, however, Harkirat Singh had been married off to a Sikh girl. Alys was heartbroken. On the rebound, she married Faiz and bore him two daughters—Saleema and Muneeza.

Faiz was no lady killer. He was of short stature, with a dark-brown complexion that looked as if he had been massaged with oil. He was a man of few words, soft-spoken and impassive. It was not his conversation but his poetry that made him the centre of attraction at every party. Besides his genius, he was remarkably free of any kind of prejudice, racial or religious, and many of his closest friends were Hindus and Sikhs. He was a humanist in the best sense of the word. There were many contradictions in his character. He was a communist but was more at ease amongst capitalists. He was a man who denied God yet was most God-fearing. In his writings, he championed the cause of the poor and the downtrodden; but his style of living was that of an aristocrat: his daily consumption of premium Scotch and imported cigarettes would have fed a worker's family for a month. However, he readily deprived himself of these luxuries to live on rations of dry bread and water given to him when he was imprisoned owing to his involvement with the Communist Party in post-Partition Pakistan.

The Partition of India left deep wounds in Faiz's mind. Although he decided to stay on in the country where he was born, he refused to accept the division between the peoples: he was unhappy with the way Punjabi-dominated Pakistan treated its eastern wing, the way Bhutto manoeuvred to deprive

Sheikh Mujibur Rahman of the prime ministership of the country and let loose General Tikka Khan army on hapless Bengalis. He remained to the end of his days Pakistani, Indian and Bangladeshi—he had as little patience with national divisions as he had for the racial or the religious.

It was Faiz's years in prison that brought out the best in him as a poet. Being in prison, he once said, was like falling in love again.

Bujha jo rauzan-e-zindaan to dil yeh samjha hai
Ke teri maang sitaron say bhar gayi hogi
Chamak uthey hain silasil, to hum nay jaanan
    hai
Kay a sahar terey rukh par bikhar gayi hogi

When light in my prison window fades and
    comes the night
I think of your dark tresses and stars twinkling
    in the parting
When chains that bind me sparkle in the light
I see your face light up with the light of the
    morning

I have little doubt that Faiz had a premonition of his death. How else can anyone interpret the last poem that he wrote?

Ajal key haath koi aa raha hai parwanah
Na jaaney aaj ki fehrist mein raqam kya hai

Death has some ordinance in its hand
I know not whose names are on the list today

Faiz's village of nativity, Kala Qadir, where he intended to spend his last days, has renamed itself Faiz Nagar. Faiz could not have asked for a better imam zamin for his journey into the ultimate.

FIRAQ GORAKHPURI

(1896–1982)

There is a gross misconception that Urdu is the
language of Muslims. There were, and there are
today, many good poets of Urdu who are Hindus.
The greatest amongst them was Raghupati Sahay,
better known as Firaq Gorakhpuri, a Kayastha from
Gorakhpur, Uttar Pradesh.

Besides being a good poet, Firaq had a creditable
academic record and had qualified for the civil
services. But he resigned to join the freedom
movement and spent some months in jail with
Jawaharlal Nehru. For four years, he was the
undersecretary of the Congress. He topped in the

MA examinations and taught English at Allahabad
University, before returing as reader in 1958. In
1961, he won the Sahitya Akademi Award; two years
later, the Soviet Land Nehru Award; and in 1970,
the Jnanpith Award. He could write in Hindi, Urdu
and English, but he opted for Urdu as the better
medium to convey his ideas. He soon came to be
sought after in mushairas, where his closest rival and
friend was an equally good poet, Josh Malihabadi
(who migrated to Pakistan after the Partition).

Firaq had a disastrous marriage. His daughter
died young, his son committed suicide, and he
wrote a lot of nasty things about his wife. His ideal
of a female companion was:

Moan aur behen bhi, aur cheheti bhi
Ghar ki rani bhi aur jeewan sathi
Phir bhi voh kaamini sarasar devi
Aur seyj par voh beswa ki petli

Mother, sister, daughter I adore
Queen of my home, life companion and more
Much desired as a goddess as well
But when in bed a voluptuous whore

Firaq was one Urdu poet who—instead of turning
to Arabic and Persian vocabulary and imagery, as

most poets of that language did—injected a lot of Hindi words in his poems. Instead of using Laila-Majnu, the bulbul, the rose, the moth and flame as symbols of eternal love, he turned to Radha and Krishna. Alongside, he used a lot of imagery from Keats, Shelley, Wordsworth and Tennyson in his compositions. He admitted openly that it often took him weeks to perfect a couple of lines of poetry.

Firaq died in Delhi in 1982 after a long illness. When he heard of his friend Malihabadi's death only a few days ago, he is supposed to have said, 'Once again, the fellow has beaten me to it.'

GEORGE FERNANDES

(1930-)

If anyone is looking for an appropriate subject for a biography, I can suggest one person through whose life one can tell the story of contemporary India, including the story of its achievements and failures: George Fernandes.

I have always had a soft spot for George. He had everything I do not have. When I first met him, he was a handsome, well-built young man with zest for life, which attracted the most beautiful of women; I was a flabby, paunchy Sardar, more seeking than sought for. The one thing we had in common was our disdain for all religions.

I have known George in different incarnations. I recall my first sight of him during a hot summer afternoon on a small platform at Kala Ghoda Chowk in the midst of hundreds of Bombay's cab drivers, exhorting them to fight for their rights. Later, the same evening, I met him at a cocktail reception given by Mota Chudasama. He was the centre of attention with all the bejewelled glitterati of Bombay's elite society and as much at ease chatting with them as he was talking to sweaty taxi drivers. He was a trade union leader then, basking in the glory of being a giant-killer, having trounced Maharashtra's leading dada-politician, S.K. Patil, in the Lok Sabha elections. At one time, he edited a weekly, *Pratipaksha*, in Marathi and Hindi; in one of its issues, he described Parliament as a brothel house. The case was taken up by the Privileges Committee. And, for reasons unknown, dropped.

When Emergency was declared, George went underground. However, he managed to let his friends know that he was still around. Once I was summoned by Mrs Gandhi to Delhi for an off-the-record and strictly private meeting; the day I got back to Bombay, I found a letter from George on my table with a one-line query: 'How did your meeting with

Madam Dictator go?' He was outspokenly critical of Indira Gandhi. A few months later, the Calcutta police nabbed him and he was brought to the Red Fort in Delhi for interrogation.

The next time I was saw George was at Palam airport. I noticed an enormous limousine flying the Indian tricolour draw up along the ramp. Members of a Russian trade delegation came down the steps; Camera bulbs flashed as they shook hands with some dignitary sent to receive them. It was the Honourable Mr George Fernandes, minister for something or the other.

I met George several times after the Janata Dal government was thrown out of power. When I asked him about his past, about his underground days as the elusive pimpernel, he said, 'No politician in India has had more bones in his body broken than I. Nor perhaps has anyone been in as many jails as I have. The police thought I was in the garb of a sadhu, so they went about interrogating sadhus. That was too obvious a camouflage. I let my beard grow and taught myself how to tie a turban. The beard grew fast enough, though the hair on the head remained short.' When he travelled around the country by air, he booked himself under my name for no better reason than he could not think of another Sikh name. 'But you can't even speak Punjabi, and here many people know me,' I said to him. He smiled and replied, 'I said I was born and brought up in Canada. And no one ever asked me whether I was Khushwant Singh.' He knew only three Punjabi words: Sat Sri Akal.

It was after several months that the police realized that George was disguised as a Sikh, when he made the mistake of staying in one place longer than he should have. A note he had sent to a friend to get money led to his arrest in Calcutta. The police wanted him to admit he was George Fernandes and not Mr Singh, which he stoutly denied. The police then tried to break him down. He was too important a politician to be subjected to the third degree, but they did their worst to frighten him. They took him into the jungle to give him the impression that they would shoot him and pass it off as having killed him in an encounter. After they brought George to the Red Fort, they changed tactics. They used the filthiest abuses. 'Ma, behen, beti, no one was spared,' George told me. 'Then they stripped me naked—a naked man feels very defenceless and betrays himself. While two officers were interrogating me, there were dozens of eyes watching every movement of mine from behind glass panels. They gave me a rough, prickly blanket to sleep on—it was like lying on a bed of nails. When none of this worked, they tried to break down my morale by other devious means.' After many hours of grilling in a hot interrogation room, they would ask George if he would like chilled beer, lemonade or ice-cream; when he would say 'Yes, thank you', nothing would come.

After the anti-Sikh violence of November 1984, following the assassination of Mrs Gandhi, I met George frequently. He set up a relief organization to rehabilitate the families of victims. I received a lot of donations from Sikhs living abroad; I passed them on to George's organization for disbursement. Then I saw George as defence minister. There was not the slightest change in his behaviour. No red light on his car, no sirens blowing, no escort.

George was never a one-woman man. I heard of many women who befriended him, including a starlet in Bangalore. One such woman I knew well was the dusky, curvaceous beauty Olga Tellis. I lost track of George for a while after he married Humayun Kabir's daughter, Leila, a Bengali Muslim;

though she bore him a son, the marriage did not work out. I saw a great deal of Jaya Jaitley, who was George's companion for twenty-five years. I had known her as a schoolgirl, when her family lived in the neighbouring block. She was the heartthrob of all the boys with her in school and college, including my son, Rahul.

There is more to George Fernandes than a swashbuckling comprador of Indian politics. Who, besides him, a South Indian, could win elections from Bihar? Who, besides him, could charm anyone he met? It is a thousand pities that he has been stricken by Alzheimer's disease. Your memory goes, you can't tell one person from another. And you gradually sink into oblivion. I know, because my wife suffered from the disease for five years before she died.

Unfortunately, a battle is raging around George now, regarding who gets to visit with him—so much so that the courts have been drawn into adjudicating whether Jaya Jaitley is allowed as a visitor or not. It is perhaps fortunate that George Fernandes, 'Giant Killer', is blissfully unaware of the bitterness around him.

GIANI ZAIL SINGH

(1916–1994)

When Giani Zail Singh was sworn in as the seventh president of India on 25 July 1980, I was rash enough to forecast that despite his modest education and inability to speak English he would prove to be the most popular president the country had had thus far—outstripping the suave Rajendra Prasad, the scholarly Radhakrishnan and Zakir Hussain, the garrulous V.V. Giri and Neelam Sanjeeva Reddy and the all-too-pliable Fakhruddin Ali Ahmad.

Zail Singh started off with a bang. On Thursday, 8 July 1980, he came to the Central Hall of Parliament to bid farewell to fellow parliamentarians and announce the termination of his long association with the Congress party. He was a few minutes late and was visibly embarrassed as Prime Minister Indira Gandhi was addressing the assemblage. She further embarrassed him with her words of welcome: 'See, he is blushing like a bride!' So Zail Singh did to the roots of his glossy-black dyed beard. His farewell speech to his fellow politicians was a tour de force of sentimental oratory, the like of which is rarely heard these days. He ended with a reference to Mrs Gandhi's quip about his blushing, admitting that he felt like an Indian bride taking leave of her parents, brothers and sisters, when every member of the family is in tears. 'You have decided to retire me from politics; however, mine will be a kind of shahi retirement,' he concluded.

Zail Singh's first few months as rashtrapati were roses-all-the-way. Wherever he went, he was welcomed by mammoth crowds. He regaled them with rustic anecdotes, Urdu couplets, Persian and Punjabi poetry, quotations from sacred Sanskrit texts, the Koran and the Granth Sahib. Here, at last, was a 'people's president'—earthy, able to talk on the same level to the peasant and the artisan; able to enter into dialogue with the pandit, the maulvi and the granthi. The only class with which he neither tried to nor was capable of making an equation with was the Westernized waggery. They cracked Sardarji jokes at his expense at their cocktail parties. He often exposed himself to their jibes, as he did when criticizing the Darwinian theory of man's descent from apes: 'How could the Buddha be a progeny of a monkey?' he naively asked. But few wags dared to take him on in public because they knew they could not hope to match him in witty repartee. He ignored their existence.

The one thing that had irked the sophisticated sections of society was Zail Singh's exaggerated deference to the 'royal family'. He had said he would be willing to sweep the floor if Mrs Gandhi so desired and acknowledged the then heir-apparent Sanjay Gandhi as his rehnuma—his guide. Few people realized that durbardari—flattery—was deeply ingrained in his psyche as he was born and brought up in the courtly atmosphere of Faridkot, where only sycophancy and cunning ensured survival.

Within a few months of his presidency, however, things began to go awry. It was Zail Singh's own community, which had earlier lauded his elevation as the first Sikh president, that began to deride him.

The Akalis launched their Dharam Yudh Morcha against the government; Zail Singh mocked them saying 'Akali, akal ke khali'—Akalis are empty-headed. They retaliated by describing him as a sarkari Sikh and the prime minister's rubber stamp.

Akali demonstrations against the ninth Asiad gave Bhajan Lal's Haryana constabulary freedom to harass all Sikhs coming to Delhi by rail and road. For the first time in the history of independent India, Sikhs came to be discriminated against. It was ironic that this should have started when a Sikh presided over the country. Zail Singh's stock amongst the Sikh community began to decline. Then events overtook him with rapid succession—Operation Blue Star was followed by Operation Woodrose to comb the Punjab countryside for terrorists.

Zail Singh had been kept in the dark about Blue Star, but the Sikhs held him responsible for it. High priests of the Takhts summoned him to explain why he should not be declared a tankhaiya. In many gurdwaras, posters with his pictures were laid out on the floor at the entrance for worshippers to tread on. His TV appearance visiting the Harmandir Sahib after the carnage, wearing a rose in his sherwani, caused a wave of resentment. He was virtually written off by his community. Then came the assassination of Mrs Indira Gandhi, followed by the massacre of Sikhs in towns and cities of northern India. Being a Sikh, Zail Singh had to suffer the odium with which Hindus began to regard his community.

Hardly had the country returned to normalcy and Zail Singh regained his equipoise than the new prime minister, Rajiv Gandhi, began to exhibit boorishness unbecoming of his lineage towards an elder to whom he initially owed his position. Zail Singh felt isolated and unwanted. I was pretty certain that he would be looking for a suitable opportunity to resign and leave Rashtrapati Bhawan with the same kind of fanfare with which he had entered it. I was wrong. He stepped out of his mansion not with the proverbial bang—but not with a whimper either.

In the last six months of his presidency, Zail Singh gave Rajiv Gandhi and his advisors a taste of their own medicine and many sleepless nights. What is more, if they had any illusions of making up for lost sleep after Zail Singh quit Rashtrapati Bhawan, they were in for a nasty surprise. Unlike his predecessors, who disappeared into pastoral oblivion after their retirement, he became a retired president living in the capital and determined to level his score with the prime minister. I foresaw Zail Singh becoming the patron saint of those disenchanted with the regime. Although he did not fulfil my prophecy of being the most popular president of India, he went down in the pages of history as the most controversial.

What was there in this man of humble origin and little academic learning that helped him overcome one obstacle after another to reach the pinnacle of aspiration and become the head of state? I will let incidents in his life speak for him.

Zail Singh was an active worker of the Praja Mandai of the erstwhile Faridkot state. The raja had personally ordered him jailed and kept him in solitary confinement. When India became independent and Faridkot was merged into PEPSU, the Central Government was looking for suitable men to run the new state. Sardar Patel summoned Zail Singh. Zail Singh did not have the money to buy a third-class return ticket from Faridkot to Delhi and had to ask friends for a loan. In Delhi, he stayed at Gurdwara Sisganj. He did not have money to hire a tonga to take him to Sardar Patel's residence at five in the morning. He walked the entire four miles and was late for his appointment. Sardar Patel's daughter brusquely dismissed him. It was the kindly secretary V. Shankar who let him see the deputy prime minister. Zail Singh was told that he was being made minister of state in PEPSU. He walked back to the railway station to return to Faridkot.

He never looked back. The remarkable thing about this man was that he did not forget his humble origins, nor did he let power go to his head. Success was to him a gift given to him by the Great Guru, not something owed to him by virtue of his abilities. One of his favourite couplets warned of the dangers of hubris:

Jin mein ho jaata hai andaaz-e-khudai paida
Hum ne dekha hai voh butt toot jaate hai

Mortals who allow notions of divinity to germinate in them
We have seen those idols shatter and come to grief

There was not even a suspicion of arrogance in the man. Besides humility, his faith in religion taught him to be honest and truthful. He was one of the breed of politicians—now almost extinct—who, though handling vast sums of money, never feathered their own nests or those of their relatives. He owned no house, flat or tract of land except the little he inherited. Nobody ever accused him of telling a lie.

As a junior minister, Zail Singh set about assiduously cultivating the support of the lower and discriminated castes. He was a Ramgarhia (carpenter) in a Punjab always dominated by Jat and Sikh politics constipated by caste considerations. He broke the Jat hegemony over the state and successfully mocked Akali pretensions of being thekedars (monopolists) of the Khalsa Panth. He was able to convince the Sikhs that he was a better Sikh than all the Akali leaders put together. His speeches were always full of quotations from the Gurbani and episodes from Sikh history. No other politician, either from the Akali party or the Congress, could build the kind of Gursikh image for himself as Zail Singh did. By the time he made his presence felt in the state, a precedent had been established that the chief minister of Punjab should be a Sikh. There was no better Sikh than Giani Zail Singh to fill the role.

Zail Singh's six-year tenure as chief minister was perhaps the most peaceful and prosperous the state had ever seen. They were the years of the Green Revolution. They were also the years without morchas, bandhs or strikes.

Zail Singh was able to rekindle pride in Punjabiyat. From England he acquired the mortal remains of Madan Lal Dhingra, who had been hanged for the murder of Curzon-Wylie, and of Udham Singh, hanged for the murder of Sir Michael O'Dwyer, Governor of Punjab at the time of Jallianwallah Bagh, and raised martyrs' memorials over them. He sought out the long-forgotten and ailing mother of Bhagat Singh, gave her a handsome grant and had her honoured as 'Punjab Mata'—Mother of Punjab. the road connecting Anandpur to Fatehgarh was named Guru Gobind Singh Marg; horses believed to be descendants of the Guru's steed were taken along the marg for the populace to see and marvel at. A new township, Baba Ajit Singh Nagar, was named after the Guru's eldest son. Massive kirtan durbars were organized all over the state. In his eagerness to wrest the Akali monopoly over the Khalsa Panth, he unwittingly set in motion a Sikh revivalism which turned into fundamentalism under Bhindranwale.

Zail Singh could not have foreseen this development, much less wished it, because his relations with Punjabi Hindus, including the somewhat anti-Sikh Mahasha press of Jalandhar, remained extremely cordial and, if gossip is to be believed, more than cordial with the smaller Muslim community. Zail Singh achieved the incredible: he had no enemies. Besides being the Punjabi paradigm of dostaan da dost—of friends the friendliest—he had the knack of winning over detractors. Even in the heyday of his power, as chief minister and home minister, he never tried to settle scores with people who had persecuted or humiliated him. He won them over by granting them favours and making them ashamed of themselves. If there was anything he could do for anyone, he never hesitated. He had an incredibly good memory for names and faces. He was able to gain friends by simply recognizing people he had met even briefly.

During the Emergency, while he had many people put in jail, he went to see them. He sent a wedding gift to Badal's daughter when he was in prison and went to receive the baraat at the house of a friend's daughter in Kalka when her father was locked up. If he heard a friend was sick, he would find time to visit him in hospital and quietly slip a bundle of currency notes under the pillow. Virtually the only man he was unable to win over was Darbara Singh, who succeeded him as the chief minister of Punjab.

To describe Zail Singh as a farsighted statesman would be an exaggeration; to describe him as a cunning politician would be grossly unfair because the stock-in-trade of a cunning politician is the ability to tell a blatant lie. And the one thing that no one could accuse Zail Singh of was falsehood. He was best as a shrewd judge of men and events. After Mrs Gandhi's murder, there were many claimants to the prime ministership; one of the senior-most civil servants of the time even suggested to Zail Singh that he take over the position himself. Sensing the anti-Sikh climate of the day, it was Zail Singh who brushed aside this suggestion and decided to offer the prime ministership to Rajiv Gandhi in the belief that, as the descendant of Jawaharlal Nehru and Indira Gandhi, he would be best suited to hold the country together.

When the opposition tried to put him up for a second term and Congress dissidents assured him of a substantial vote from the party, Zail Singh carefully weighed his prospects before turning it down. He was not a gambler; he played to win.

It was the same when pressure was brought on him to dismiss the prime minister or permit his prosecution on charges of corruption. Zail Singh had little to lose and could have made things very hot for Rajiv Gandhi. But he refused to succumb to temptation—teaching Rajiv a lesson for his bad behaviour—because he felt that the nation's future was paramount and India was more important than Zail Singh or Rajiv Gandhi.

After Operation Blue Star, I requested a meeting with Giani Zail Singh in order to return my Padma Bhushan to register my protest. When the appointment was granted, I saw that he was in a state of acute depression. 'I know how you feel,' he said to me. 'But don't be hasty. Think about it for a few days and then decide what you should do.' I held my ground: 'No, Gianiji. I don't want to give myself time to change my mind. I had sworn that if the army entered the temple I would renounce the honours bestowed on me by this government.' Even after the citation was put aside, Zail Singh continued talking to me. 'I don't think my qaum'—community—'will ever forgive me for this,' he said, looking for some kind of assurance to the contrary. 'No, Gianiji,' I replied, 'I don't think the Sikhs will ever forgive you for Blue Star.' He looked to be in the depths of despair. 'Do you think it would serve any purpose if I resign now?' he asked. I told him that it was too late: whether or not he resigned, the Sikhs would hold him responsible for the desecration of their holiest shrine.

Zail Singh often quoted a couplet to the effect that, while he put a rose in the palms of Rajiv Gandhi, Rajiv took a stone to hurt him. There is another equally apt couplet that perhaps best encapsulates Giani Zail Singh's political career:

Zakhmi huey jo hont toh mehsoos yeh hua
Chooma tha maine phool ko deevangi ke sath

It was the bruises on my lips that made me comprehend
With what thoughtlessness I had kissed the rose

INDER SAIN JOHAR

(1920–1984)

Inder Sain Johar was a few years younger than me. He was in Forman Christian College, Lahore, and was making some noise on the amateur stage as a comic actor. We had met, shaken hands, but did not get to know each other. One summer evening, when I was a practising lawyer living in a small flat opposite the high court, I heard a band playing raucous music coming down the road. I went to my balcony to see what was happening. It was a wedding procession. On a white horse sat I.S. Johar, decked up as a bridegroom. He was on his way to marry Rama Bans, a very pretty girl who also acted in college plays. The couple migrated to Bombay to try their fortune in the film industry. I lost track of them.

Johar and Rama had two children, a son and a daughter. I saw some films in which Johar had acted, including a couple of Hollywood productions in English. I did not rate him a great actor. When he turned from acting to directing films, in which he cast himself in the main role, I formed an even poorer opinion of his histrionic talents. When he ran out of ideas, he descended to shocking people. In one film (I think it was *Five Rifles*), he had his own daughter appear bare-breasted on screen. I don't recall how he got around the censors. His wife, Rama, was disillusioned and divorced him to marry a cousin named Harbans and opened a health cum beauty parlour in Delhi. She was even more disillusioned with her second husband, sold her business and returned to Bombay. Her son had by then become a dope addict. Her daughter made a disastrous marriage with an Englishman who abducted their only child and smuggled him away to England. Johar had by then had many liaisons.

Rama took on the job of the manager of the health club at the Taj. She regained her youthful vitality and good looks. Since I went to the club every day for exercise and a sauna bath, I became very friendly with her. She even persuaded me to take facial massages, which I found deliciously sensuous. Rama had by then resumed some kind of undefined relationship with her first husband. Johar had a keen eye for publicity. Rama used to visit him once every week. When Johar discovered that she had befriended me, he asked her to bring me over to his apartment in Lotus Court. I was then editing *The Illustrated Weekly of India*. For many months, I was a weekly dinner guest at this set-up.

After my sauna bath, Rama and I would proceed to Lotus Court. Rama then rang up Johar, who was at the Cricket Club of India, playing bridge. She told him to bring some Chinese food from the club restaurant. I played with his miniature Penkingsee bitch named Pheeno, 'the snub-nosed'. Snub-nosed she certainly was, and very cuddlesome. Rama would sometimes open the drawers of Johar's bedside table (he always slept on the floor) and pull out stacks of pictures of young girls in bikinis—or less. They were of girls looking for jobs in films. Johar would arrive carrying cartons of Chinese dishes and get out a bottle of premium Scotch for me. Neither he nor Rama touched alcohol. I had my quota of three drinks before we ate dinner. Then Rama dropped me at my apartment and went home. I never got to know where she lived. All I was able to gather was that she had ditched her second husband, but I was not sure whether or not she had patched up with Johar. I often pulled her leg about being the only Indian woman I knew who could claim to have two husbands at one time.

Johar sent me the manuscript of his autobiography for serialization in *The Weekly*. It was difficult to tell how much of it was factual, how much the creation of his sick fantasies. In any case, there was more sex in it than was permissible for journals at the time. If Johar was to be believed, he started his sexcapades at the age of twelve. He was spending his vacation with his uncle and aunt who had no children of their own. One night, he had (or pretended to have) nightmares and started whimpering in his sleep. His aunt brought him to her bed. He snuggled into her bosom and soon had an erection. He tried to push it into her. She slapped him and told him to behave himself. The next morning, he was afraid he would be scolded and sent back home. However, his aunt was sweetness itself. After her husband had left for his office, she offered to bathe him. While she was soaping him, he again got sexually aroused. This time his aunt taught him what to do with it. It became his daily morning routine. Nevertheless, Johar confessed that in the years of his adolescence what he enjoyed most was being buggered by older boys.

The autobiography did not mention Rama. But in the years after their separation, he wrote of a starlet (who later became a star I won't name) whom he set up in a flat in Malabar Hill. Whenever he felt like it, he would drop in on her, have a drink or two and then bed her. One evening, he was in a particularly horny mood. When he got to the lady's flat, he was informed by her young Goan maidservant, 'Memsahib baahar gaya.' Madam has gone out.

'Kab ayega?' When will she return?

The maid replied: 'Kya maloom? Bahut late hoga.' Who knows? She will be very late.

So Johar simply pushed the girl on the bed and mounted her. The girl protested: 'Memsahib ayega toh hum bolega.' When Madam returns, I will tell her. At the same time, she opened her legs to her mistress's paramour.

Even more bizarre was his story of how he bedded

two sisters and their mother. One sister had been his mistress for some years before she left him to get married. She introduced her younger sister to Johar and asked him to help her get into films. He not only got her a few minor roles but also asked her to stay in his flat. One evening, she came back from the studios looking very tired. Johar asked her if she would like a hot cup of tea or something stronger to cheer her up. She replied, 'If you really want to know what I would like best, I'd like a nice fuck.' The girl left Johar to become a star. Her mother wrote to Johar to thank him for what he had done for her daughters and asked him if she could stay with him for a couple of days when visiting Bombay. One night, she came to his bed, stark naked. 'I did not want to hurt the old lady's feelings,' wrote Johar, and 'obliged her the same way I had obliged her daughters.'

How could I have published these memoirs without inviting the wrath of the proprietors of the journal on my head?

Johar accused me of cowardice; I accused him of making up stories. The less work he got, the more stories he made up.

One day, he rang up and asked me to come to his

flat with a cameraman. 'I'm getting engaged to be married later,' he told me.

'To whom?' I asked.

'To Protima Bedi,' he replied.

Protima had two grown-up children by Kabir Bedi. She had not yet made a name as an Odissi dancer, but had gained wide publicity by streaking on Juhu beach. The pictures of her running across the sands without a stitch on had appeared in many papers. She had a most fetching figure. Johar was at least thirty years older than her, a grandfather in daily communication with his ex-wife, Rama. However, I went along with my photographer.

There were dozens of photographers and press people present. Johar was dressed in a beige silk kurta-pyjama, with his hair freshly dyed jet-black. Protima was decked up in a bridal sari, with a lot of gold jewellery on her. With one eye, you could see that this was a publicity lark for both of them. The next morning's papers had them on their front pages.

They were back in the news. No marriage followed. Johar talked no more about Protima Bedi.

I had a farewell dinner of sorts before I left Bombay for good. It was like old times. Rama, Pheeno and me, with Johar joining us later with Chinese food. By now, Pheeno had taken to snuggling in my lap and grunting with contentment. 'She seems to be fonder of you than me,' remarked Johar. 'Would you like to take her?' I agreed to accept Pheeno. I would take her with me to Delhi to my family, every one of whom was passionately fond of animals. 'It is like having to give my daughter away. I can't do it,' Johar said by way of explanation. I understood his feelings.

I continued to communicate with Rama long after Johar went out of my life. All said and done, I was fonder of her than her ex-husband. However, I felt a pang of anguish when I read of Johar's death in Bombay. And I wondered what became of Pheeno.

INDIRA GANDHI

(1917–1984)

In 2009, the twenty-fifth death anniversary of Indira Gandhi occasioned a flood of literature and huge media coverage across the country. That was as it should have been because she was, in fact, the Queen Empress of India for long years and changed the face of the country by ruthless plastic surgery. She made the Congress subservient to her wishes, nationalized banks, deprived princely families of their unearned privy purses, inflicted a humiliating defeat on Pakistan and liberated Bangladesh. Dev Kant Baruah was not much off the mark when he hailed her thus: 'India is Indira, Indira is India.

Tere naam ki jai! Tere kaam ki jai!' However, it must not be forgotten that there were two distinct sides to her character—the public persona, and the private. She was a great public leader, but at the same time she was very petty in her private life. She was undoubtedly a most beautiful woman, but she disliked other good-looking women and humiliated them, among whom were Tarakeshwari Sinha and Maharani Gayatri Devi. And the number of people she and her family put behind bars during the Emergency makes one sick. But she was able to get away with what she did because India's poor millions loved her as 'Amma'—Mother.

I first met her when she was still unmarried and had stopped in Lahore on her way to Kashmir. I must have been about eighteen years old then. Indira was staying with friends who brought her over to our house. She appeared very shy and would not talk much. I remember thinking of her as a 'goongi gudiya'—a mute doll. Years later, when I met her in Delhi, she did not seem to recollect that meeting, though I have pictures of her at our house.

Indira Gandhi was a very good-looking woman— not the pin-up kind but an indescribable aristocratic type. She reminded me of Hilaire Belloc's lines:

Her face was like the King's command
When all the swords are drawn

I have been asked if I ever wanted to get close to
her in the physical sense; the answer is no. There
was something cold and haughty about her. Not
my type at all, for I like women who are vivacious
and spontaneous. But she had her set of admirers.
Amongst the many men who were bowled over by
her looks was President Lyndon Johnson of the
United States. Just before a dinner hosted by the
Indian ambassador B.K. Nehru and his wife for
Indira, at which Vice President Hubert Humphrey
was to be the guest of honour, Lyndon Johnson
stayed on tossing glass after glass of bourbon on
the rocks while talking to Indira. He readily agreed
to stay on for dinner, to which he had not been
invited. At a reception at the White House, Lyndon
Johnson asked her to dance with him; she refused
on the grounds that it would hurt her image in
India. The president understood. He wanted to see
'no harm [come] to the girl' and sanctioned three
million tons of wheat and nine million dollars of
aid to India.

The only person on record who made derogatory

references to Indira's looks and intelligence was her aunt, Vijaya Lakshmi Pandit. Indira never forgave her (or her daughters) for slighting her and denied her senior diplomatic assignments. Indira Gandhi never forgave anyone who said anything against her.

Indira Gandhi's greatest triumph was the way she handled the Bangladesh crisis, wherein all her skills came together. She made a complete fool of the Pakistanis. India was being flooded by refugees entering the country. She tried to garner international support and went around the world, telling people what was happening. When she realized that the crisis had to reach a climax, she proved very astute. It was perhaps on her advice that the Indian Army built up the Mukti Bahini. By the time that President General Yahya Khan realized what was happening and declared war, the Indian Army was well inside Bangladesh. In less than a fortnight, the Pakistani Army surrendered. It was, by all accounts, a masterful strategy, and Indira Gandhi very deservedly got the Bharat Ratna.

At the end of the crisis, *The Illustrated Weekly* was the only Indian journal to persist in pressuring the government to release the 93,000 Pakistani prisoners of war. I took a delegation of four members, including

one-time Indian ambassador to the US Gaganbhai
Mehta and the writers Khwaja Ahmed Abbas and
Krishan Chandra, to call on Indira Gandhi in an
attempt to facilitate the release of the prisoners.
Mrs Gandhi snubbed Gaganbhai, calling him an
American stooge, and silenced Abbas and Chandra.
Then she turned on me and said that my writings
were embarrassing her. I replied that the object of
my exercise was indeed to embarrass her and I was
glad to know that I was succeeding. She fixed me
with a look of contempt and said, 'Mr Singh, you
may regard yourself as a great editor. But let me tell
you, you do not know the first thing about politics.' I
said, 'Mrs Gandhi, what is morally wrong can never
be politically right. Holding prisoners of war after
the war is over is morally wrong.' She again turned
her large, dark eyes on me. 'Thanks for lecturing
me on morality,' she said and dismissed us. I was
convinced that she would never speak to me again.
But a few days later, when she was in Bombay, she
sought me out at a large and crowded reception and
chatted with me in a friendly manner. I knew then
that I had driven my point home.

In 1975, with accusations of corruption in the
government soaring and the opposition calling for

total revolution, the country was fast sliding into
chaos. Every other day, there was a bandh of some
kind. Schools and colleges stayed shut for days. Large
processions marched through streets, smashing
shop windows and wrecking cars. Indira Gandhi
was driven to despair. Her position became further
vulnerable when the Allahabad high court held
her guilty of electoral malpractices and disqualified
her from Parliament membership. Persuaded by
advisors such as Siddhartha Shankar Ray and Sanjay
Gandhi, she imposed Emergency on the country.
My attitude to the Emergency was ambivalent. I
supported the move to clamp down on law-breakers
(including Jayaprakash Narayan, whom I otherwise
admired), but I felt that the censorship of the press
would prove counter-productive as it would deprive
editors like me, who supported Mrs Gandhi, of
credibility. For three weeks, I did not publish
The Illustrated Weekly and, when forced to resume
publication, gave instructions that no photographs
of Mrs Gandhi or her ministers were to be used. I
was treated gently, as I was regarded as a friend by
Mrs Gandhi and Sanjay, and summoned to Delhi
to meet her. I had my say, protesting against the
censorship, and told her before leaving, 'My family

is sure that if I spoke my mind you would have me locked up.' She smiled and bade me goodbye. *The Weekly* was treated as a special case and I published articles by critics of the Emergency and pleaded for the release of political prisoners.

There was, as I have said, a strong streak of vengefulness in Indira Gandhi. A lot of people who were jailed during the Emergency were victims of the spite of the Gandhis. Despite repeated requests and pleas for the release of such prisoners, Mrs Gandhi refused to relent—including in the case of Bhim Sain Sachar, ex-chief minister of Punjab, then in his seventies. One thing that Indira Gandhi did not suffer from was compassion. Her pettiness was particularly evident in her dealings with her younger daughter-in-law, Maneka. After Sanjay—whom Mrs Gandhi both loved and feared—died, she made Maneka unwelcome in her home and showed a marked preference for Sonia.

Another characteristic she developed after years of being in power was to snub people who least expected to be. At my repeated requests, she agreed to see Kewal Singh, who had been her foreign secretary and ambassador in Washington. Then she proceeded to give him a dressing down till he broke down. She did the same to Jagat Mehta, whose posting as ambassador to Germany she cancelled after it had been accepted.

When it came to Operation Blue Star, I believe Indira Gandhi was misled. From my years of acquaintance with her, I know that she had no prejudice at all against any community—not against Muslims, not against Sikhs. She consulted people about handling Bhindranwale and got contradictory advice from different sides. She didn't trust President Zail Singh, so she turned to the army. She was assured by senior officials that once the army went in and surrounded the Golden Temple, no fight would be put up and Bhindranwale would surrender. I know that when she went to the temple two or three days after the operation, she was horrified because bodies were still floating in the sarovar and there were bloodstains that were being cleaned up. She turned to Major General K.S. Brar and asked, 'What is all this?' She had believed the army when she was told that there would be no fighting.

I was still a Member of Parliament when Mrs Gandhi was assassinated on the morning of 31 October 1984. Despite my differences with her, I was deeply distressed to hear of her dastardly murder at

the hands of her own security guards, both Sikhs.
She had many shortcomings, but perhaps that alone
was what made her human. She may not have been
a likeable person, but she was, in her own way, a
woman to be loved and admired.

JARNAIL SINGH BHINDRANWALE

(1947–1984)

Through the 1970s and '80s, Hindu-Sikh tensions continued to bedevil the Punjab. They came to a head with the rise of Sikh fundamentalism under Jarnail Singh Bhindranwale, who led terrorist activities aimed against Punjabi Hindus in the early 1980s.

In an attempt to get better acquainted with Punjab politics, I decided to go to Amritsar on the day the Akalis launched their Dharam Yudh Morcha in 1982. I had strong reservations about it. In the morning, I met leaders of the Congress and the BJP. In the afternoon, I walked up to the Manji

Sahib Gurdwara adjoining the Golden Temple to listen to Akali leaders and take in the scene. There must have been over 20,000 Sikhs sitting on the ground and another five to ten thousand standing around. On the dais, beside the Granth Sahib, sat the elite of the Akali party: Sant Harcharan Singh Longowal, Jathedar Tohra, ex-chief minister Prakash Singh Badal, ex-finance minister Balwant Singh, ex-Members of Parliament Balwant Singh Ramoowalia and Nirlep Kaur, as well as the sitting MP Rajinder Kaur. The shining star of the galaxy was Jarnail Singh Bhindranwale.

Tohra spotted me standing in the crowd and sent two men to fetch me. Very reluctantly, I allowed myself to be dragged along and found myself seated in the front row between the Granth Sahib and the microphone. Most of the speeches that followed were directed at me. I find it very painful to sit on the ground and had to keep shifting my position to give relief to my aching knees and bottom. As one fiery speech followed another, the crowd became restless and clamoured for Bhindranwale. At last he came to the microphone, amid thunderous cries of 'Boley So Nihal—Sat Sri Akal!' He was a tall, lean man with an aquiline nose, fiery eyes and a long, flowing beard. In his left hand he held a silver arrow, the sort seen in pictures of Guru Gobind Singh and Maharaja Ranjit Singh. A bandolier charged with bullets ran across his chest. He had a pistol attached in its holster and held a four-foot-long kirpan in his right hand.

Bhindranwale had never seen me. I heard him turn to one of his cronies and ask: 'Eh kaun hai?'— who is he? I heard my name mentioned. He knew about me and what I had written against him. I had issued instructions that the prefix sant (saint) was not to be used with his name in any reference to him in the paper I edited. An Australian pressman had told him that I thought that Bhindranwale was aiming to become the eleventh Guru of the Sikhs. 'If that fellow really said that,' Bhindranwale had replied, 'I will have him and his family wiped out.' The Australian had quickly recanted in order to save our lives.

Like those of the others, Bhindranwale's speech too was addressed to me. 'I don't know this Sardar Sahib sitting near my feet,' he started. 'They tell me he is the editor of some English paper called the *Hindustan Times*. I can't speak English. I am told he writes that I create hatred between Sikhs and

Hindus. This is a lie. I am a preacher. I go from village to village, telling Sikhs to come back to the path of the tenth Guru. I tell them to stop clipping their beards, to refrain from taking opium and smoking tobacco, I baptize them into the Khalsa Panth.' There were loud cries of 'Sat Sri Akal' to express approval at this. Bhindranwale warmed to his theme. 'If I had my way, you know what I would do to all these Sardars who drink whisky-shisky every evening? I would douse them in kerosene oil and set fire to the bloody lot.' The announcement was greeted with prolonged cries of 'Boley So Nihal—Sat Sri Akal'. It was ironic that the vast majority of the audience applauding him were Sikh Jats notorious for their addiction to hard liquor. I turned to Badal and Balwant Singh, both of whom had taken Scotch at my home and said, 'What Chief Minister Darbara Singh has been unable to do with all his police, this chap will do with one matchstick.' They sniggered.

Over time, Bhindranwale's speeches became more acerbic and contemptuous of Hindus. He would refer to Mrs Indira Gandhi as 'Panditan di dhee' or 'Bahmani'—'that Pandit's daughter' or 'the Brahmin woman'. Hindus were 'dhotian, topian waley'—'those who wear dhotis and caps'. In one speech, he exhorted every Sikh to kill thirty-two Hindus—not thirty-one, not thirty-three, only thirty-two, he said—in that way, the entire population of Hindus would be accounted for.

Through the course of my attempts to document the recent history of the Punjab and Sikhs, the one thing I have been unable to understand to my satisfaction is the phenomenon of Bhindranwale. When he first burst onto the Punjab scene, I had dismissed him as one of the hundreds of rustic preachers who are found all over a countryside where sants are a dime a dozen. By the time he entrenched himself in the Golden Temple complex and launched his anti-Hindu tirades, I was describing him as a 'demented hate-monger'. I do not know why more Sikhs did not denounce him as a homicidal maniac.

During the days when he was making his hateful utterances, I called on Sant Longowal, nominal head of the Dharam Yuddh Morcha, in his room in the offices of the SGPC. The meeting did not yield much copy; I sensed that he was unhappy with Bhindranwale but was unable to do anything about him. Bhindranwale was entrenched in the Akal Takht, and his armed bodyguards had the run of the Golden Temple complex and were more than eager to bump off anyone their leader wanted out of the way. I asked Longowal why he allowed Bhindranwale to say nasty things about Hindus from the sacred precincts of the Akal Takht. Longowal replied, 'O tay saada danda hai'—he is our stave [to hit the Congress government with].

The Bhindranwale chapter in Indian history is a perfect illustration of the disastrous results of not keeping politics separate from religion. Jarnail Singh Bhindranwale was a creation of the Congress and the Akalis. Indira Gandhi was advised by President Zail Singh that this small-time 'kattar'—hardline Sikh preacher—should be built up as a leader to counter the ruling Akalis in Punjab. But soon enough, the Akalis tried to woo Bhindranwale away from their rivals and propped him up. In time, he became a monster who would turn around and destroy the very people who created him and plunge Punjab and much of the country into chaos.

How is it that a man who had so little to say that made sense and said so much that was hateful came to gain so much popularity? The Congress tried to exploit his popularity; so did the Akalis. Both parties were thoroughly mauled by him. Longowal's 'saada danda' belaboured both the Akalis and the Congress government.

Perhaps the most plausible explanation of the Bhindranwale phenomenon comes from a compilation of essays, *Punjab Today*, edited by Gopal Singh of Himachal University. A paper on Sikh revivalism by Pritam Singh of Punjab University gives the background of the conditions which made the Bhindranwale phenomenon possible. Believe it or not, most of it was due to the prosperity that came with the Green Revolution. With prosperity came degeneration—the spread of uncontrolled alcoholism, smoking, drug addiction, gambling, pornography, fornication. The worst sufferers of this degeneration were women and children—wives and offspring of peasants who could not smoothly digest their prosperity. On this scene arrived Bhindranwale, preaching against such Western evils and carrying on a vigorous campaign of 'Amritprachaar'.

Bhindranwale's popularity among Sikhs has an interesting lesson for our times, when Hindu fundamentalists are becoming increasingly popular among middle-class Hindus who are materially better off now than they have ever been.

Everywhere he went, Bhindranwale baptized

Sikhs by the thousands and made them swear in front of congregations that they would never again touch alcohol and drugs and so on. These baptized Sikhs did not break their oath. Money previously squandered was saved. Time previously wasted in drunkenness or being stoned was spent on more careful tillage—bringing more money. It was the women and children, their menfolk suddenly reformed, who first acclaimed him as a saviour and a saint. To this image, Bhindranwale added the macho gloss of a tough man: bandolier charged with bullets across his hairy chest, pistol at his hip, in his hand a silver arrow. The crowds loved him when he mocked Indira Gandhi and referred to the Central Government as 'bania-Hindu sarkar'. Unemployed young men who passed out of college but could not be absorbed into their ancestral farming business were impressed by his fiery speeches and became his followers.

When Bhindranwale shifted to the Golden Temple and his goons began killing innocent people, his admirers dismissed the allegations as government propaganda—to them, he was a good guy. Even as Hindus were being pulled out of buses and shot and transistor bombs were going off in crowded markets all over northern India, Sikh pride was at its height.

As tension mounted in Punjab and the killing of innocents at the behest of Bhindranwale increased, the Central Government realized that its options were closing; it had to somehow get hold of Bhindranwale again (he had been arrested earlier on charges of murder and released at a time and place of his choosing). By now, Bhindranwale and his military advisor, General Shahbeg Singh, had converted the Akal Takht into a fortress and a variety of arms had been smuggled in by trucks carrying rations for the gurdwara kitchen. The government had left it too late, and a violent confrontation was fast becoming inevitable.

On many occasions, I warned the government against sending the army into the Golden Temple because it would rouse the wrath of the entire Sikh community. 'You don't know the Sikhs,' I once told Home Minister P.C. Sethi, a peace-loving Jain. 'They can be like a swarm of hornets. You put your head in their nest and you will be stung all over your face.' He assured me that the government had no intention of sending the army into the temple. So did Mrs Gandhi, more than once.

It is not known for sure when Mrs Gandhi came around to the view that she had no option but to order the army into the Golden Temple, and who her advisors were at the time—though the names of Rajiv Gandhi, Arun Nehru, Arun Singh and Digvijay Singh have come up. There is no doubt that President Zail Singh was kept in the dark. When Mrs Gandhi persuaded him to put Punjab under military rule, she did not tell him that she had decided to order the army to clear the temple of Bhindranwale and his armed followers—when it came to Punjab or Sikh affairs, she did not trust Gianiji.

It is also unknown who chose the date when operations should commence. Without the foggiest notion of Sikh traditions, they settled on 5 June 1984 as the day to launch the operation—it was the death anniversary of Guru Arjun Dev, the founder of the Harmandir Sahib, a day when hundreds of thousands of Sikhs were expected to come on pilgrimage from remote areas.

Alternative methods of getting at Bhindranwale were not considered seriously. He could have been overpowered by a band of commandos in plain clothes; the temple complex could have been cordoned off; the people inside deprived of rations and access to potable water and forced to come out into the open to surrender or be picked up by snipers. It would have taken a couple of days longer but would have been comparatively bloodless.

As it happened, the army stormed the Golden Temple with tanks, armoured cars and frogmen, with helicopters hovering overhead to give directions. The battle that ensued lasted two days and nights. In the crossfire, almost 5,000 men, women and children perished. The Akal Takht was reduced to rubble by heavy gunfire; the central shrine, which both parties had declared hors de combat, was hit by over seventy bullets; the entrance had a large portion blasted off; archives containing hundreds of handwritten copies of the Granth Sahib and hukumnamas (edicts) issued under the signatures of the Gurus were reduced to ashes. Even Mrs Gandhi, who had been assured that the operation would not last more than two hours, was horrified at the extent of damage caused to sacred property and the horrendous loss of lives.

I regarded Bhindranwale as an evil man who deserved his fate. But Operation Blue Star went well beyond the slaying of Bhindranwale: it was a calculated and deliberate slap in the face of an entire community. Despite my indifference, and even hostility, to religion, I had no doubt in my mind that I should reaffirm my identity with my community—I decided to return my Padma Bhushan to the government.

In light of the Indian Army's actions, I was willing to concede that Bhindranwale had met his end like a warrior, but I also heaved a sigh of relief—I hoped that we had heard the last of him. But I was wrong.

A few months later, on 31 October 1984, Indira Gandhi was slain by one of her Sikh bodyguards. Terrible results followed. In towns and cities across the Indo-Gangetic plain and down to Karnataka, frenzied mobs, often led by Congress leaders, took a heavy toll of Sikh life and property. In Delhi alone, over 3,000 Sikhs were burnt alive and over seventy gurdwaras wrecked.

For years, Jarnail Singh Bhindranwale's portrait at the Golden Temple has drawn large crowds. Photographs of him and cassettes of his speeches sell by the thousands. To a sizeable section of Sikhs, he has become an 'amar shaheed'—eternal martyr—who laid down his life for the Khalsa Panth.

He continues to be venerated as Sant Baba Jarnail Singhji Khalsa Bhindranwale.

It will not be easy to exorcise Bhindranwale's ghost from the Punjabi mind.

JAWAHARLAL NEHRU

(1889–1964)

Pandit Jawaharlal Nehru, it must be said, fully answered the poet Allama Iqbal's requirements of a Meer-e-Kaarvaan—leader of the caravan:

> Nigah buland, sukhan dilnawaz, jaan par soz
> Yahi hain rakht-e-safar Meer-e-Kaarvaan ke liye

> Lofty vision, winning speech and a warm personality
> This is all the baggage the leader of a caravan needs on his journey.

Nehru should have been the role model for the prime ministers of India. He was above prejudices of any kind: racial, religious or of caste. He was an agnostic and firmly believed that religion played a very negative role in Indian society. What I admired most about him was his secularism. He was a visionary and an exemplary leader; the father of Indian constitutional democracy, of universal adult franchise, the five-year plans and giving equal rights to women, among other things. He was better educated than any of his successors, with the exception of Manmohan Singh, and spent nine long years in jail reading, writing and thinking about the country's future.

But being human, Nehru had his human failings. He was not above political chicanery. Having accepted the Cabinet Mission Plan to hand over power to a united India, he reneged on his undertaking when he realized that Jinnah might end up becoming prime minister. Nehru had blind spots too. He refused to believe that India's exploding population needed to be contained. He refused to see the gathering strength of Muslim separatism, which led to the formation of Pakistan. He failed to come to terms with Pakistan and was chiefly responsible for the mess we made in Jammu and Kashmir. He was also given to nepotism and favouritism. And his love affairs with Shraddha Mata and Lady Mountbatten are well-known. I have been often asked whether the central character of my novel *Burial at Sea* was based on Nehru— you could say that the inspiration for the character was Nehru.

I first met Nehru in London, when I was a press officer at the Indian Embassy, and my first impression of him was that he was short-tempered. He could also be ill-mannered. I once had to host a lunch so that the editors of leading British newspapers could meet him. Halfway through the meal, Nehru fell silent. When questions were put to him, he looked up at the ceiling and did not reply. He then proceeded to light a cigarette while others were still eating. To make matters worse, Krishna Menon fell asleep. It was a disastrous attempt at public relations.

Another time, Nehru arrived in London past midnight. I asked him whether he would like me to accompany him to his hotel. 'Don't be silly,' he said. 'Go home and sleep.' The next morning, one of the papers carried a photo of him with Lady Mountbatten opening the door in her negligee. The photographer had taken the chance of catching them, if not in flagrante delicto, at least in preparation of it, and got his scoop. The huge caption read: 'Lady Mountbatten's Midnight Visitor'. Nehru was furious. On another occasion, he had taken Lady Mountbatten for a quiet dinner at a Greek restaurant. Once again, the following morning's papers carried photographs of them sitting close to each other. Our prime minister's liaison with Lady Edwina had assumed scandalous proportions, and I knew I was in trouble.

I arrived at the office to find a note from Krishna Menon on my table, saying that the prime minister wished to see me immediately.

I gently knocked on the prime minister's door and went in. He was busy going through some files.

'Yes?' he said, raising his head.

'Sir, you sent for me. '

'I sent for you? Who are you?'

'I am your PRO in London, sir,' I replied.

He looked me up and down. 'You have a strange notion of publicity,' he said curtly.

I thought it best to remain silent.

KRISHNA MENON

(1896-1974)

After the Partition, I found myself back in London
with a job as an information officer with the public
relations department of India House. I was to stay
with Arthur and Sheila Lall in Knightsbridge until
my family arrived and we found a place of our own.
Arthur was very taken with Krishna Menon. He
assured me that Krishna Menon was the finest brain
he had ever met and compared favourably with
Stalin (who was not known to have a particularly
fine brain). I had briefly met Krishna Menon in
my college days and had not detected any signs of
genius in him. He was a sour-tempered barrister

without briefs and spent his energies building up his India League and paying court to Pandit Nehru whenever he was in England. His appointment as high commissioner was badly received in India and the Indian community in England; people considered it gross favouritism. But after hearing Arthur go on about him, I thought I had perhaps been wrong in my estimate of Menon, or perhaps he had matured into a better man.

I reported for work at India House and introduced myself to Sudhir Ghosh. He didn't seem very pleased to see me. Beneath the glass slab of his working table were a number of photographs and originals of letters exchanged between Gandhi and Sir Stafford Cripps, Gandhi and Prime Minister Attlee, all praising Sudhir Ghosh. It was quite evident that Sudhir was having trouble with Krishna Menon and was not on good terms with Indian journalists. He showed me to the tiny cubicle I was to occupy and introduced me to an English girl, Pamela Cullen, who was to be my assistant. He did not tell me what I was to do. 'You can ask Menon when you meet him,' he said. He studiously avoided calling Menon high commissioner, or even adding a mister to his name.

I had no idea what public relations meant, nor what I was to do to promote them. Not having been briefed or charged with a specific task, I decided that perhaps the best I could do was produce booklets on India—its people, resources, flora, fauna, etc. For the first four days after my arrival in London, I reported for work at India House every morning. I signed the visitors' book and reminded Sudhir Ghosh to introduce me to the high commissioner. He didn't think it was urgent. I asked Arthur. He said it was not for him but Sudhir to do so. However, he told Menon that I had wanted to call on him. On the fifth day, Sudhir Ghosh took me up to Menon's room.

I had a broad grin on my face when I greeted Krishna Menon and extended my right hand. He brushed it aside with his claw-like fingers. Instead of a smile of welcome, he had an angry frown on his face. I cheerfully reminded him that I had once travelled with him and Rajni Patel to Paris. He ignored my self-introduction and barked, 'Sardar, haven't they taught you any manners in India? You have been here four days and haven't had the courtesy to call on me. I am the high commissioner, you know!' My smile froze. I protested I had done my best—signed the visitors' book, and asked both Sudhir Ghosh and Arthur Lall to get me an appointment. Sudhir interrupted to say that it was his fault. 'I'll send for you later,' said Menon, dismissing me. 'I want to speak to Mr Ghosh.'

I returned to my cubicle very shaken. No one had ever spoken to me the way Menon had done and without any reason whatsoever. I was determined not to put up with it. I swore to myself that the next time Menon said anything harshly I would hit back, put in my letter of resignation and tell him to stuff it up his dirty bottom. I was out of sorts all afternoon. Instead of doing any work, I took a long stroll along the Thames embankment till my temper came down a little.

In the evening, there was a tea party in the main reception room. I went, took a cup of tea and sat down in a corner. Menon breezed in; I pretended not to have seen him. He came up to me and put his arm around my shoulders. 'Sorry for ticking you off this morning,' he said. 'I hope you had the sense to realize it was not meant for you.' I stood up, somewhat flabbergasted at the change of tone. 'I was a little taken aback,' I replied. 'If you don't have that much common sense, you'll never do as an information officer,' he said to me. He then patted me on my back and went to shake other hands. I was utterly deflated. The fellow obviously meant to be friendly towards me; it was Sudhir Ghosh he was gunning for. Menon had a convoluted mind.

It did not take me long to get a hang of India House politics. Krishna Menon had his coterie of faithfuls. At the top of the list was Arthur Lall, his trade commissioner. His other favourites were junior members of his staff; some, like his personal secretary, Captain Srinivasan of the Indian Navy, he savaged till they proved their loyalties to him. Menon had scant respect for the deputy high commissioner, R.S. Mani, also of the ICS and his number two man. Mani was a flabby man with a flabbier Belgian wife. He did his best to ingratiate himself with Menon and suffered being treated like a doormat—he remained a doormat. Menon was also allergic to men in uniform and treated his military, naval and air force attachés with unconcealed contempt. His bete noire was Sudhir Ghosh, who was determined to run the public relations department as an independent establishment of his own.

Sudhir regarded himself as Gandhi's personal envoy to well-meaning Britons who had sided with the freedom movement. Most of them were Quakers. He entrusted them with official missions without consulting Menon. 'Let Menon do his job and let him leave me alone to do mine,' he often told me as he gloated over the photographs and letters on his table. 'I have spent many years with Gandhiji. I have no hatred in my heart against anyone,' he assured me over and over again. Then he resumed his tirade against Menon.

Menon had an eye for good-looking women. He treated the husbands of good-looking women as friends. If he sensed tension between the couple, he became especially considerate towards them—he had great understanding for misunderstood wives. Sheila Lall and my wife (after the family joined me) fell in that category. Arthur and I became his number one and number two favourites. But topping us was young Kamla Jaspal, who had joined his clerical pool.

Kamla was a Sikh—light-skinned, with curly black hair and a charming squint in one eye. She came to office dressed as if she were going to a cocktail party. She wore bright-coloured chiffon saris, with blouses that left most of her middle, including her belly button, exposed. She wore bracelets of silver, gold and glass; they covered most of her forearms and jingle-jangled whenever she brushed her untidy locks from across her face, which was often. Being scantily clad, she often caught colds and had a running nose. She dropped names of English poets, and she danced a few steps of Bharatanatyam badly; she also wrote bad prose and poetry. She was loud and aggressive in asserting herself. But she worshipped Krishna Menon as if he were an incarnation of Lord Vishnu. Like a good Hindu wife she never referred to him by his name or as high commissioner but as HE—His Excellency. To Krishna Menon, who had been away from India for several decades, Kamla Jaspal represented modern Indian womanhood. He responded to her adoration with flowers and favours, including the use of his Rolls Royce to take her home. He was tiring of his ageing English mistress, Bridgette, who looked after the India League, and was on the lookout for a replacement. For a while Kamla courted Bridgette and soon discovered that she could oust her. In India House, everyone knew that in order to get on with Krishna Menon one had to get on with Kamla Jaspal. During that posting in London, I cultivated both Bridgette and Kamla.

Menon had reason to trust me more than Sudhir Ghosh and decided to use me as an instrument to get rid of him. He did not have to wait long for the opportunity to do so. I first discovered how bad things were when I chanced to see a confidential letter Menon had written to Pandit Nehru. He described Ghosh as a 'Patelite'. Evidently, Nehru's relations with his deputy prime minister, Sardar Patel, were strained. He also argued that foreign publicity should be under the foreign minister (Nehru) and not under the home and information minister (Patel). Before Panditji could respond to this letter, the incident of the missing chit occurred, which proved Sudhir Ghosh's undoing.

One morning, Menon sent a note to Sudhir Ghosh on a scrap of paper in his own hand, asking him to send me up to see him as soon as I reached the office. Sudhir took no notice of it till a couple of hours later, when Kamla Jaspal came down to check whether or not I had arrived. I went to Sudhir's office to find out what it was about. 'Oh, yes, Menon wants to see you without me,' he said, reading the chit. He crumpled it and threw it into his wastepaper basket. When I went to see Menon, he asked me why it had taken me two hours to come up. I told him I had known nothing about it till Kamla told me and I had then gone to Sudhir's room. Sudhir was summoned. He blankly denied having received any message from Menon. I left them going at each other, returned to Sudhir's room and pulled out the crumpled chit from his wastepaper basket. Through Kamla Jaspal, I had the chit handed over to Menon. I do not know how the Gandhian Sudhir got out of the blatant lie he had told. The next day, he left for India; Menon followed him a few days later.

While they were away, I received telegraphic orders transferring me to Canada. P.L. Bhandari, whom I had known as a junior reporter with *The Civil and Military Gazette* of Lahore and who regarded himself as an expert in public relations, was named Sudhir's successor. A few days later, Menon and Sudhir returned to London. The latter made only one appearance in India House, to take away his pictures and testimonials from his table. His parting kick was to host a large luncheon party at the Savoy Hotel for his English friends. He did not bother to invite me or any other colleagues. At that one party, he blew up the entire year's entertainment allowance of the public relations department.

Menon was a complex character—the most unpredictable and prickly I have ever met. I had first met him on the London-Paris train when he and Rajni Patel were on their way to attend some conference. At Dover, he and Rajni jumped the queue of passengers awaiting immigration clearance. When the immigration officer told them to go back to the line, Menon accused him of racial prejudice. The fellow let them through. Menon had a chip on his shoulder about being 'a black' and picked quarrels on imaginary racial insults. For a time, he had worked as a waiter at restaurants to pay for his studies at the Bar. He never picked up any practice but got to know socialist politicians and was on the panel of editors of the Pelican series of books. Till he became high commissioner, he was always very hard-up and eager to accept any hospitality extended to him.

Menon was slim, middle-sized and dark, with sharp features and bright, shining eyes. He had a broad forehead, his curly black hair greying at the temples, a large nose and high cheekbones. Women found him handsome. He was very tense; his face was never at rest and twitched with animation. He was always very well-dressed, in suits made by a well-known firm of tailors; he could not bear others being badly dressed. Once he cancelled his morning appointments, took me to his tailor, chose the material and had me measured for two suits. I thought he meant to gift them to me and thanked him profusely. They were not gifts; I had to shell out several hundred pounds. But they were the best suits I had and lasted me over twenty years. Menon was not generous with his money, except when it came to his lady friends and children; even then, it was seldom more than bouquets of roses for the one, cheap plastic toys for the other.

Menon lived frugally in a room alongside his office. He ate very little but filled himself with cups of sugared tea and salted biscuits. However, he did not mind blowing up large sums of money buying a Rolls Royce for the high commissioner (that is to say, himself) and a fleet of Austin Princesses for the use of Indian visitors and India House officials. With his limited requirements, he had no need to accumulate wealth; nevertheless, he did so. He didn't spend a penny of his salary but set up many sub-organizations of his India League and got money from rich Indians and his English friends as donations to those organizations; in return, he gave them contracts for the supply of arms to India. He had no scruples in business matters. He was also a congenital liar and regarded truth as good enough for the simple-minded and lying as the best exercise for the mind.

Menon's first reaction to any proposal put to him was to reject it. Those who got to know him better learnt to put their proposals in the negative and invariably got his approval by his rejection of them. He built up a reputation of being a workaholic. He kept long hours, which he wasted on trivialities such as checking the menus of the canteen and the consumption of petrol by the office cars. He forced me to sleep in the office on many nights. There was never enough work to justify imposing this discomfort on me. He knew that I was very keen on games and looked forward to Saturday afternoons, when I played tennis or hockey. Without fail, he would ring me up before lunch on Saturdays and ask me to attend some meeting he was holding in the afternoon. He had a strong streak of sadism.

Menon's bad temper and discourtesy had to be experienced to be believed. As with many men, he was at his worst in the mornings, before his gastric juices started flowing. I saw him hurling a file in the face of Jagannath Khosla and yelling: 'Have you any brains in your head? Get out!' Then he put his head between his hands to cool off and asked me, 'I shouldn't have spoken to him like that, should I have?' I conceded he had been a little rough with a senior officer. He summoned Khosla back and apologized. Khosla replied, 'Sir, it is a privilege to be ticked off by you.' One morning, when Menon failed to get a long-distance call, he screamed at the operator. The plucky English girl shouted back: 'Don't you dare talk to me like that! I am quitting. You can keep your bloody job.' Menon ran down the stairs, put his arms around the angry girl and apologized. Once I brought David Astor, the owner-proprietor of *The Observer*, and his aide William Clarke to meet Menon. He called the English a race of brigands. On the way down, in the elevator, David remarked to me: 'You must have quite a job doing public relations for Menon!' His deputy, Ashok Chanda, knowing Menon's predilection for denying anything he said if he later found it embarrassing, insisted that he put all his orders in writing. He often breezed into my office and triumphantly announced: 'Hum shala ko phaeel mein aisa mara! Bhoolega nahin'—I gave the fellow whose sister I fuck such a hiding in the file, he'll never forget it. Sir Dhiren Mitra, our legal advisor, never lost his cool; he continued placidly puffing his pipe and dismissed Menon with: 'Paagal hai'— he is mad.

Those who silently suffered Menon's tantrums were handsomely rewarded. Of them the most dramatic was the instance of Brigadier Harnarain Singh and his wife, Rani. Menon took an instant dislike to the brigadier. The latter described himself as the chief of Moron, a small zamindari near Phillaur in the Punjab. Menon always addressed him as the 'chief of the morons'. The brigadier did not know what the English word meant and would protest in his nasal whine: 'Sir, who cares for such titles these days!' His wife also liked to be treated as an aristocrat. She was the daughter of Sardar Sohan Singh, a wealthy landowner of Rawalpindi; her name, Rani, confirmed her aristocratic assumptions. Menon got to know that she had been spreading scandal about his affair with Kamla Jaspal. He summoned her to the office, roundly ticked her off and called her a bitch. A very tearful Rani craved forgiveness. Thereafter, the couple assiduously courted Kamla Jaspal and became Menon's favourites. Another two senior officers who were treated like scum but accepted their treatment without protest were Captain Srinivasan and D.N. Chatterjee. Srinivasan, a married man with children, impregnated his attractive English stenographer. It was after Menon had extracted many pounds of flesh off the hapless naval captain that he allowed him to divorce his Indian wife, marry the vastly pregnant English girl—and retain his job. Chatterjee had divorced his Bengali wife (one of Lord Sinha's progeny) and wanted to marry a Belgian heiress. By the rules of the Foreign Service, he was required to submit his resignation before his application could be considered. Chatterjee had to suffer months of humiliation before Menon forwarded his application with the recommendation that it be accepted. Chatterjee retired as an ambassador.

Merit did not matter very much to Menon; unquestioned loyalty did. He persuaded the prime minister to constitute a panel to interview applicants living in England for the Foreign Service. He got Harold Laski appointed chairman with him and someone else to constitute it. The panel selected P.N. Haksar (the only one who merited selection), Jagannath Khosla, Kamla Jaspal and Rukmini

Menon (a clerk and the sister of a junior officer in the military attaché's department). Later, Menon also managed to get Keki Darashah and Prithi Singh, who had an English wife, in the subordinate Foreign Service. He held out similar promises to me; he would have me elected to Parliament and perhaps made a minister in the government. But my days as a Menon favourite were fast drawing to a close.

Menon was never rude to me. For many months, I enjoyed special favours and my colleagues who wanted things done by him used me as their via media. I travelled with him to distant towns in England where he was invited to speak. Kamla Jaspal briefed me on his personal requirements. Amongst items I had to carry were bottles of lemonade: he drank a glass for his nightcap. Though his English was heavily Malayali-accented, Menon was a witty speaker. He was full of acid wit and sarcasm against the English and people who could not retaliate. At his first meeting with senior army, navy and air force officers training in England, he addressed them as 'Macaulay's children'. He did not enjoy other speakers scoring over him and could be quite childish in the ways in which he got the better of them. Once, speaking at the Convention of Master Cutlers at Leeds, he was at his acid best and extracted much laughter from his audience—the English enjoy laughing at themselves. Unfortunately for Menon, the chief host who rose to propose the vote of thanks turned out to be a better orator than Menon; his jokes and anecdotes got even louder applause. I saw Menon beckon a waiter and ask for another cup of tea. As the speaker was building up to a climax, Menon raised his cup with a shaking hand. Just as the speaker was about to deliver his punch line, Menon dropped the cup from his hand and spilt tea all over the table. The punch line remained undelivered and the banquet came to an abrupt end.

My most memorable venture with Menon was a visit to Dublin, where we were to open an embassy—Ireland's first full diplomatic mission. Menon decided to take his defence attachés and their wives with him. I was included in the party and asked to bring my wife along. Our party was received at Dublin airport with a guard of honour and we were put up in Dublin's swankiest hotel. The next morning, Menon was to present his credentials to the Irish president.

My phone rang early in the morning. It was a very sick-sounding Menon asking me to come to his room at once. I found him groaning in bed.

'I am very sick,' Menon moaned. 'Cancel all the day's engagements.'

I was aghast. 'Sir, they must have made a lot of preparations. Let me get the hotel doctor and see what he had to say.'

'Can't you see I am a sick man?' he growled.

I got the hotel doctor. He could not diagnose anything wrong with Menon except that he might be suffering from exhaustion. Menon was inconsolable. 'Get the chief of protocol on the line.' While I was trying to get the right number, we heard the stamp of marching feet come to a halt beneath our window. 'What is that?' asked Menon. I looked out. 'Soldiers drawing up. I expect they are to escort you to the Presidential Palace.' Menon began to feel better. He went to the bathroom to shave and brush his teeth. When he came out, we heard the sounds of a military band down the road and coming to a halt outside the hotel. Menon had a quick look from his window. He got into a black sherwani and churidar and told me, 'Sardar, go and get dressed. We don't have much time.' Menon was now in great form. We were taken in a convoy led by a band and a troop of soldiers. Curious Dubliners lined the roads and Menon waved to them. The credentials were presented and accepted.

President Douglas invited Menon to his home for a cup of tea in the afternoon and Menon asked me and my wife to accompany him. We were led to a book-lined study with a peat fire smouldering in the grate. The president made polite enquiries about India; Menon launched into a long harangue about India's mineral and hydro-electric resources, its industries and agricultural potential. The president listened in silence. At the end of his long monologue, Menon asked the president how Ireland was faring. 'Nothing much worth the talking,' drawled President Douglas. 'We don't have much to export, except invisible items like poets, novelists and dramatists.'

That evening, we held a reception for the Irish president, prime minister and leaders of the Irish opposition. Amongst those who turned up was Eamon De Valera. Following classical music, as we were being shown to our box, an announcement came over the loudspeaker that Ireland's first foreign ambassador had arrived. The audience rose to applaud him. A beam of light searched the crowded hall to pick up Menon. Instead of him, it focused on me—with my turban and beard, I looked more authentically India than anyone else in our party. I tried to dodge the beam by going to the back row, but the beam pursued me. Menon enjoyed my discomfiture and kept pushing me to the front. No one was able to acknowledge the applause of the audience.

Nothing specific happened to sour my relations with Menon. Of the two women he was close to, over time I became friendlier with Bridgette, who was very distressed by Menon's infatuation with Kamla Jaspal. She regarded Kamla as a designing seductress who had brought Menon a bad name. I made the mistake of saying this to Menon; he snubbed me and told me to mind my own business. Then some comment on Kashmir appeared in *The Manchester Guardian*. Menon and Haksar drafted the reply; it was sent to me for my signature as the press attaché. I could have drafted a similar reply—and perhaps have phrased it better—but I was not even consulted. The correspondence continued in the paper. In all, I signed three letters I had not written. I felt slighted and let my hurt be known to everyone in the office. Then, instead of talking to me directly, Menon began to convey his orders through Kamla Jaspal. I told her not to bring messages to me as I was always available to the high commissioner on the phone. Menon accused me of being rude to Kamla; his infatuation at the time was at its peak.

The time had come to bid a final farewell to India House. When I went to say goodbye to Jamal Kidwai, who had taken my place, he told me that Menon wanted to give a farewell reception for me. I told him flatly that I wanted no reception and did not wish to see Menon. He pleaded with me and said that he would give the reception and Menon would come only for a few moments. I knew Menon would do nothing of the sort, but agreed to go to Kidwai's party. Reluctantly, I also went to see Menon. He was courteous and said that despite our misunderstanding he regarded me as a friend. 'You don't have any friends,' I told him bluntly as I left. As I had anticipated, Menon did not turn up at the farewell reception. Kidwai apologized on his behalf to say that Menon was unwell and confined to his bed. But I saw him go briskly down the steps and get into his Rolls Royce—lying was Menon's second nature and came as easily to him as discourtesy.

Why Menon got where he did under the patronage of Pandit Nehru remains, and probably will remain, unexplained. Panditji had him elected to Parliament and sent him to the United Nations to lead the Indian delegation. His marathon thirteen-hour speech on Kashmir won India a unanimous vote against it. He was then made defence minister against the wishes of almost all the members of the Cabinet. He wrecked army discipline by promoting favourites over the heads of senior officers. He was vindictive against those who stood up to him. More than anyone else, he was responsible for the humiliating defeat of our army at the hands of the Chinese in 1962. And yet, Pandit Nehru stuck by him to the last.

The last time I spoke to Menon was on the telephone. I happened to be in London working at the India Office Library. I was sharing a flat with Sheila Lall and we had a common telephone. Every night, she would be out with one of her many lovers. The telephone would ring, but when I would pick up and say 'hello' the line would go dead. I complained to Sheila. 'That must be Krishna,' she told me. 'He wants me to be his mistress—no strings attached.' The next time the telephone rang, instead of saying the customary 'hello' I spat out with venom: 'You bloody bastard, I know who you are! Stop ringing up at this hour or you will hear worse.' There were no calls after that.

Menon is the subject of a couple of biographies and a road is named after him. I think in my long years I got to know him better than his biographers or any of the leftists who acclaim him as a great son of India. General Shiv Varma summed him up aptly when he said, 'Menon was a bachelor, the same as his father.'

LAL KRISHNA ADVANI

(1927–)

My worry today is the rise of right-wing fascist parties in the country. The youth of today should be aware of the rise in communal politics and the dangers involved. If we love our country, we have to save it from communal forces. And though the liberal class is shrinking, I do hope that the present generation totally rejects communal and fascist policies. I shun people who are at the forefront of this communalism, and this includes the likes of L.K. Advani.

When I had first met Advani, I thought he was forthright and clean and able. So we kept in touch. In 1989, he chose me to file his papers for nomination to Parliament, and I supported him by proposing his name as MP from New Delhi. I set my hopes on him because Sikhs were targeted by the Congress in 1984 and Advani seemed to be the only choice. Advani cashed in, and there were photos and banners and what not. But my disillusionment began when he started fouling the atmosphere of the country.

The one event that pitchforked Advani to the centre stage and reshaped India's politics was his rath yatra from Somnath to Ayodhya, leading to the destruction of the Babri Masjid on 6 December 1992. He, more than anyone else, sensed that Islamophobia was deeply ingrained in the minds of millions of Hindus; it only needed a spark to set it ablaze. The choice of Somnath as the starting point and Ayodhya as the terminal one was well-calculated. Mahmud Ghazni had destroyed the temple at Somnath; Ayodhya was believed to be the birthplace of Sri Ram—it was bruited about that a temple to mark the birth site had stood there till Babar destroyed it and built a mosque over the ruins. This is disputed by historians and the matter was being pursued in law courts. Advani ignored legal niceties and arrived with great fanfare at the site. Since he was determined to build a new Ram temple at the same spot, the fate of the mosque was sealed. What happened there on that fateful day was seen on television by millions of people round the globe. And repercussions were felt over the world. Hindu and Sikh temples were targeted by irate Muslims from Bangladesh to the UK. There were communal confrontations in different parts of India: the serial blasts in Bombay, the attack on the Sabarmati Express in Godhra, the massacre of innocent Muslims in Gujarat—they can all be traced back to the fall of the Babri Masjid. Relations between Hindus and Muslims have never been the same in India. However, the BJP reaped a rich harvest, won many of the elections that followed and eventually installed Atal Behari Vajpayee as prime minister and L.K. Advani as his deputy.

Advani claims that breaking the mosque was not on his agenda; that he actually sent Murli Manohar Joshi and Uma Bharati to plead with those who went on the rampage to desist. If that is so, why were the two seen embracing each other and rejoicing when the nefarious task was completed? We don't need the verdict of the Liberhan Commission to tell us what happened—we saw it with our own eyes. And, in his memoir, Advani recorded the jubilation that followed at the site, along with his triumphal return to Delhi. At an event at the IIC, I told Advani to his face, in front of an audience, 'You have sowed the seeds of communal disharmony in the country and we are paying the price for it.'

The one time Advani faltered in his steps was when he visited Karachi and praised Jinnah's speech to the Pakistan Constituent Assembly on 11 August 1947 as 'a classic exposition of a secular state'. It might well have been so, but Jinnah's speech was delivered at a time when millions of Hindus and Sikhs were being driven out of Pakistan or being slaughtered, and an equal number of Muslims were being driven out of India. It was a bloody exchange in which over a million died and over ten million were uprooted. Advani's eulogy must have pleased Pakistanis; it was badly received in India, particularly by his colleagues in the RSS and the BJP.

Advani should have left the political scene in a blaze of glory; but not many tears will be shed for him now. And for good reasons. Did he ever regret the role he played in the demolition of the Babri Masjid? If he did, as he claims, why did he not tender

an apology? Did he regret the anti-Muslim pogrom
in Gujarat? If so, why did he protect Narendra Modi
from being sacked, as Prime Minister Vajpayee
evidently wanted? It was a symbiotic relationship
between the two—Modi helped Advani win elections
from Gandhinagar; Advani, in turn, exonerated
him from the anti-Muslim pogrom charges of 2002.
Is it possible that as home minister Advani did not
know of Jaswant Singh's mission to Kandahar to
swap three jihadi militants for 150-odd Indians held
hostage in hostile territory? There cannot be an
iota of truth in his statement that he knew nothing
about Jaswant's mission till it was over. Advani once
described Manmohan Singh as 'nikamma'—useless.
It so happens that Manmohan is still very much
in use, whereas Advani's own erstwhile colleagues
have pronounced him of no use any longer.

Advani has done grievous harm to our efforts to
create a truly secular India. I have no regret over his
discomfiture and eventual fadeout from national
politics—it will be as comic a tragedy as any we have
witnessed in recent times.

LOUIS MOUNTBATTEN

(1900–1979)

The last Viceroy and first Governor General
of India, Louis Francis Albert Victor Nicholas
Mountbatten, First Earl Mountbatten of Burma,
was the man charged with overseeing the transition
of British India into independent India. Two brief
encounters with him—one in London, followed
by another a few months later in Toronto—have
stayed in my mind. At the time I did not have the
nerve to put my reactions in print: he was the Lord
of Destiny, an awe-inspiring figure about whom
singing anything but paeans of praise would have
sounded discordant. However, Philip Ziegler's

excellent biography assures me that I wasn't wrong in suspecting that the emperor had no clothes. Or wore flimsy, see-through raiment.

The first meeting was unscheduled. Lord Mountbatten was the chief guest at a reception in India House. By some error, he turned up fifteen minutes before he was expected and even the host, Krishna Menon, was not present to receive him. I rushed down to greet him, apologized for the misunderstanding and suggested that he relax in my temporary office, which in any case was reserved for his wife and bore the plaque 'Countess Mountbatten of Burma'. His Lordship was out of countenance. He had come splendidly attired in an admiral's deep-blue uniform splattered with gold epaulettes, ribbons and a chestful of medals. Instead of making a spectacular entry at a glittering reception as he had planned, he was having to waste time with a nondescript clerical type. I asked him about the Partition and the stormy days that followed; he answered me in bored monosyllables.

I tried to provoke him: 'Lord Mountbatten, many people feel that if you had not forced the pace the exchange of populations might have been smoother and we might have been spared the enormous bloodshed that took place. '

At this, His Lordship was needled into replying: 'I don't give a damn about what my critics say today... I will be judged at the bar of history.'

I was taken aback by Mountbatten's pomposity. However justified, I did not expect a sophisticated English gentleman of breeding to air assumptions of immortality. It wasn't pucca.

The next encounter revealed yet another facet of Lord Louis's character. He was to inaugurate an international trade fair in Toronto, and his speech was punctuated with allusions to his royal connection. 'My cousin the king', 'my cousin the queen's consort', 'my uncle the duke of someplace or the other', etcetera, etcetera. I remember very little of what else he said.

Was there anything of substance to this man? I am not sure.

MADHAV SADASHIV GOLWALKAR

(1906–1973)

As I think on the communal beast that threatens
India today, I realize that part of the Sangh Parivar's
success over the years can be attributed to the charm
and charisma of many of its leaders. They were
men of polite manners, obvious sophistication and
intelligence who cloaked their fascist ideas in sweet
reasonableness, with impeccable etiquette.

I met Madhavrao Sadasivrao Golwalkar, the
then head of the RSS, around forty years ago. Guru
Golwalkar had long been at the top of my hate list
because I could not forget the RSS's role in communal
riots and the assassination of Mahatma Gandhi,

and its attempt to change India from a secular state to a Hindu rashtra. There were passages in his 1939 tract, *We, or Our Nationhood Defined*, that seemed to suggest that Golwalkar shared Hitler's ideas about racial purity and approved of his methods to purge Germany of Jews. I could thus not resist the chance of meeting him in November 1972 and interviewed him for *The Illustrated Weekly*.

I expected to run into a cordon of uniformed swayam sevaks. There were none. Not even plainclothes CIDs to take down the number of my car. I arrived at what looked like a middle-class apartment. It seemed as though there was a puja going on inside—there were rows of sandals outside, the fragrance of agarbatti, the bustle of women behind the scenes, the tinkle of utensils and crockery. I stepped inside.

It was a small room. In it sat a dozen men in spotless white kurtas and dhotis—all looking newly washed as only Maharashtrian Brahmins can manage. And there was Guru Golwalkar—a frail man in his mid-sixties, black hair curling to his shoulders, a moustache covering his mouth, a wispy grey beard dangling down his chin. He wore an inerasable smile and dark eyes twinkled through his bifocals. He looked like an Indian Ho Chi Minh. For a man who had only recently undergone surgery for breast cancer, he seemed remarkably fit and cheerful. Being a guru, I had imagined that he might expect chela-like obeisance. But he did not give me the chance. As I bent to touch his feet, he grasped my hand with his bony fingers and pulled me down on the seat beside him.

'I am very glad to meet you,' he said. 'I had been wanting to do so for some time.' His Hindi was very shuddh.

'Me too,' I replied clumsily. 'Ever since I read your *Bunch of Letters*.'

'*Bunch of Thoughts*,' he corrected me. He did not want to know my views on it. He took one of my hands in his and patted it. 'So?' He looked enquiringly at me.

'I don't know where to begin. I am told you shun publicity and your organization is secret.'

'It is true we do not seek publicity, but there is nothing secret about us. Ask me anything you want to.'

'I read about your movement in Jack Curran's *The RSS and Hindu Militarism*. He says...'

'It is a biased account,' interrupted Golwalkar.

'Unfair, inaccurate. He misquoted me and many others. There is no militarism in our movement. We value discipline—which is a different matter.'

I told him that I had read an article describing Curran as the head of CIA operations in Europe and Africa. 'I would never have suspected it,' I said naively. 'I have known him for twenty years.'

Golwalkar beamed a smile at me. 'This does not surprise me at all.' I did not know whether his remark was a comment on Curran being part of the CIA or my naiveté.

'There is one thing that bothers me about the RSS,' I said to him. 'If you permit me, I will put it as bluntly as I can.'

'Go ahead.'

'It is your attitude towards the minorities, particularly the Christians and the Muslims.'

'We have nothing against the Christians except their methods of gaining converts,' said Golwalkar. 'When they give medicines to the sick or bread to the hungry, they should not exploit the situation by propagating their religion to those people. I am glad there is a move to make the Indian churches autonomous and independent of Rome.'

'What about the Muslims?' I said.

'What about them?' Golwalkar countered.

'I have no doubt in my mind that the dual loyalties that many Muslims have towards both India and Pakistan is due to historical reasons, for which Hindus are as much to blame as they. It also stems from a feeling of insecurity that they have been made to suffer since the Partition. In any case, one cannot hold the entire community responsible for the wrongs of a few.' I had begun to get eloquent. 'Guruji, there are six crores of Indian Muslims here with us. We cannot eliminate them, we cannot drive them out, we cannot convert them. This is their home. We must reassure them, make them feel wanted. Let us win them over with love...'

'I would reverse the order,' Golwalkar interrupted. 'As a matter of fact, I would say the only right policy towards Muslims is to win their loyalty by love.'

I was startled. Was he playing with words? Or did he really mean what he said?

He qualified his statement: 'A delegation of Jamat-i-Islami came to see me. I told them that Muslims must forget that they ruled India. They should not look upon foreign Muslim countries as their homelands. They must join the mainstream of Indianism.'

'How?'

'We should explain things to them. Sometimes one feels angry with Muslims for what they do, but then Hindu blood never harbours ill-will for very long. Time is a great healer. I am an optimist and feel that Hinduism and Islam will learn to live with each other.'

Tea was served. Guruji's glass mug provided a diversion. I asked him why he didn't drink the beverage out of porcelain like the rest of us.

He smiled. 'I have always taken it in this mug. I take it with me wherever I go.'

Golwalkar's closest companion, Dr Thatte, who had dedicated his life to the RSS, explained: 'Porcelain wears off and exposes the clay beneath. Clay can harbour germs.'

I returned to my theme. 'Why do you pin your faith on religion when most of the world is turning irreligious and agnostic?'

'Hinduism is on firm ground because it has no dogma. It has had agnostics before; it will survive the wave of irreligiousness better than any other religious system.'

'How can you say that?' I argued. 'The evidence is the other way. The only religions that are standing firm and even increasing their hold on the people are those based on dogma—Catholicism and, more than Catholicism, Islam.'

'It is a passing phase,' replied Golwalkar. 'Agnosticism will overtake them; it will not overtake Hinduism. Ours is not a religion in the dictionary sense of the word; it is a dharma, a way of life. Hinduism will take agnosticism in its stride.'

I had taken more than half an hour of Golwalkar's time by now. But he showed no sign of impatience. When I asked for leave, he again grasped my hands to prevent me from touching his feet.

As has become abundantly clear in the past decades, the RSS is blatantly and fiercely anti-Muslim and anti-Christian. It junks Jesus just as it rejects roza. Golwalkar even raised an objection when Abdul Hamid and the Keelor brothers were honoured by the Indian government for their bravery during the Indo-Pak war—the gallant men were non-Hindus.

I remember being impressed with Guru Golwalkar in 1972 because he did not try to persuade me to agree with his point of view. Instead, he made me feel that he was open to persuasion. I even accepted his invitation to visit him in Nagpur and see things for myself. I had thought then that I could perhaps bring him around to making Hindu-Muslim unity the main aim of his RSS. I had been a simple-minded Sardar.

MAHATMA GANDHI

(1869-1948)

In the study in my cottage in Kasauli, I have two pictures of people I admire the most—one of them is Mahatma Gandhi. I admire Bapu Gandhi more than any other man. Of all the other prophets of the past we have no knowledge. Almost everything about them is myth or miracle. With Gandhi, we know—he walked among us not long ago and there are many people alive, like me, who have seen him. He was always in the public eye. He bared himself; no one was more honest.

I don't accept his foibles. He took a vow of celibacy in his prime, but without consulting his wife, which

I think was grossly unfair. He would sleep naked beside young girls to test his brahmacharya. He could be very odd. But his insistence on truth at all times made him a Mahatma. And the principle of ahimsa—not to hurt anyone. Ahimsa and honesty should be the basis of all religion, of every life.

I have been a regular drinker all my adult life. I celebrate sex and cannot say that I have never lied. I have not hurt anyone physically, but I think I have caused hurt with my words and actions. And sometimes there is no forgiveness in me. But I consider myself a Gandhian. Whenever I feel unsure of anything, I try to imagine what Gandhi would have done, and that is what I do.

If only Mahatma Gandhi were alive today, the whole situation of the country would have been different. I don't believe the likes of Anna Hazare can do a thing about corruption in India—his fasting is to no avail. Only Mahatma Gandhi would have been able to arouse mass consciousness to halt the tide of corruption and chaos spreading around us today.

I became a Gandhi bhakta at a young age. I first saw Bapu when I was six or seven years old, when I was studying at Modern School. He had come on a visit. All of us children—there were very few students in the school in those days—sat on the ground in the front row. Bapu bent down and tugged my uniform playfully.

'Beta, yeh kapda kahan ka hai?' he asked. Where is this cloth from?

'Vilayati,' I said with pride. It was from abroad.

He told me gently, 'Yeh apne desh ka hota toh acchha hota, nahin?' It would have been good had this been from our country, wouldn't it?

Soon after, I started wearing khadi. My mother used to spin khaddar, so it was easy. I continued wearing khaddar for many years. Before I went to London to attend university, I took some khaddar to our tailor because I had been told I would need a proper English suit. The tailor laughed and told my father, who asked me to stop being a khotta.

Mahatma Gandhi was only the one person who seemed to comprehend the very seriousness of the Partition and all that would follow. He did not take part in any of the independence celebrations. When anti-Pakistan feelings were at a fever pitch and the Indian government refused to honour its pledge to pay Pakistan fifty-five crores, the Mahatma went on a fast and forced the government to abide by its word. He knew he was asking for trouble but did not give it a second thought. A calumny was spread about his having agreed to the Partition of India along communal lines. He told his secretary Pyarelal: 'Today I find myself alone. Even the Sardar [Patel] and Jawaharlal Nehru think that my reading of the situation is wrong and peace is sure to return if the Partition is agreed upon... I shall perhaps not be alive to witness it, but should the evil I apprehend overtake India and her independence be imperilled, let it not be said that Gandhi was party to India's vivisection.'

I was still in London when Mahatma Gandhi was assassinated in Delhi on 30 January 1948. I had taken leave to pack my belongings to proceed to Canada. We were invited to lunch by Sir Malcolm Darling, the retired income tax commissioner who lived in a basement flat near Victoria station. As we came out into the cold, windy day after lunch, I noted scribbled in hand on a placard by a newspaper stall the message: 'Gandhi assassinated'. I did not believe it could be our Bapu. Who could kill a saintly man who had harmed no one? I asked the stall holder. He had tears in his eyes as he handed me a copy of *The Evening Standard*. 'Yes, mate, some bloody villain's got him,' he said. Tears also welled up in my eyes. I was only able to read the headlines. Instead of going on to the shipping office to confirm our passage, we made our way to India House to be with our people. Oil lamps had been lit at the base of Gandhi's portrait. The smell of aromatic incense pervaded the place. Men and women sat on the floor chanting Gandhi's favourite hymns. 'Vaishnav jan toh tainey kaheeye jo peed paraie jaane rey'—know him only as man of God who feels the suffering of others; and 'Ishwar Allah terey naam, sab ko sanmati dey Bhagwan'—Ishwar and Allah are but names of the same God, may His blessings be on us.

Bapu was pretty certain that he would not be allowed to live. At a prayer meeting on 16 June 1947, he said, 'I shall consider myself brave if I am killed and if I still pray to God for my assassin.' As he had anticipated, the assassin finally got him the following year. He went with the name of Ram on his lips—a glorious end to a glorious life.

MANZUR QADIR

(1913-1974)

Whenever anyone asks me 'Who influenced your way of thinking the most?' I answer without hesitation: Manzur Qadir. Not many people in India would have heard the name of Manzur Qadir. Even in Pakistan, where he was born and is buried, most people will have heard of him as an eminent lawyer who was made foreign minister by President Ayub Khan and then chief justice of the Supreme Court. Only a small group of friends knew him as a human being. I was among that handful of people who had the privilege of being his close friends in the years we lived in Lahore.

Our friendship continued after the Partition too. Manzur took over my house and had all my books, furniture and even empty bottles of whisky sent to me. At considerable risk to his life, he dropped my Sikh servant across the border when inter-communal strife was at its worst. Since our children were about the same age and went to college in England at the same time, the close association between the families continued for many years.

Manzur was a short, bald, beady-eyed man. He was by no means handsome; and yet, men and women were drawn towards him like moths to a flame. Though he was an average student in school and college, within four years of starting practice in Lyallpur, he was acknowledged as the most up-and-coming lawyer in the Punjab. By the time he shifted to Lahore to practise at the high court, he was recognized as the best lawyer at the Bar. He was fluent in English as well as in Urdu. Though born a Punjabi, he avoided speaking the language. He had a passion for Urdu poetry and could reel off Iqbal by the hour. He also composed bawdy verse and recited it with great gusto to a purely male audience; he was extremely proper and prudish in the company of women.

What was great about Manzur Qadir? Two things. He never said a hurtful thing about anyone. And he never told a lie. Within a short span of people knowing him, he became a kind of touchstone to judge the rights and wrongs of every course of action. We would often ask ourselves: 'Will Manzur approve of this?' Such a combination of ability, integrity, consideration and kindness I have never found in any other human being.

Whenever I visit Lahore, one of my top priorities is to visit Manzur's grave, stew rose petals on it, recite the Fatiha—he, like me, was an agnostic—and shed some tears.

MOTHER TERESA
(1910-1997)

It has been more than thirty years since I was asked to do a profile of Mother Teresa for the *New York Times*. I wrote to Mother Teresa seeking her permission to call on her. Having got it, I spent three days with her, from the early hours of the morning to late at night. Nothing in my journalistic career has remained as sharply etched in my memory as those three days with her in Calcutta.

Before I met her, I read Malcolm Muggeridge's book on her, *Something Beautiful for God*. Malcolm was a recent convert to Catholicism and prone to believing in miracles. He had gone to make a film on Mother Teresa for the BBC. They first went to the Nirmal Hriday Home for dying destitutes close to the Kalighat temple. The team took some shots of the building from outside and of its sunlit courtyard. The camera crew was of the opinion that the interior was too dark and they had no lights that would help them take the shots they needed. However, since some footage was left over, they decided to use it for interior shots. When the film was developed later, the shots of the dormitories inside were found to be clearer and brighter than those taken in sunlight. The first thing I asked Mother Teresa was if this was true.

'But of course,' she replied. 'Such things happen all the time.' Then she added with greater intensity: 'Every day, every hour, every single minute, God manifests Himself in some miracle.'

She narrated other miracles of the days when her organization was little known and always short of cash. 'Money has never been much of a problem,' she told me. 'God gives through His people.' She told me that when she started her first school in the slums, she had no more than five rupees with her. But as soon as people came to know what she was doing, they brought money and other things.

The first institution she took me to was Nirmal Hriday. It was in 1952 that the Calcutta Corporation had handed over the building to her. Orthodox Hindus were outraged. Four hundred Brahmin priests attached to the Kali temple gathered outside the building. 'One day, I went out and spoke to them. "If you want to kill me, kill me. But do not disturb the inmates. Let them die in peace." That silenced them. Then one of the priests staggered in. He was in an advanced stage of galloping phthisis. The nuns looked after him till he died.' That changed the priests' attitude towards Mother Teresa. Later, one day, another priest entered the home, prostrated himself at her feet and said, 'For thirty years, I have served the Goddess Kali in her temple. Now the Goddess stands before me.'

On my way back, Mother Teresa dropped me at the Dum Dum Airport. As I was about to take leave of her, she said, 'So?' She wanted to know if I had anything else to ask her.

'Tell me, how can you touch people with loathsome diseases like leprosy and gangrene? Aren't you revolted by people filthy with dysentery and cholera vomit?'

'I see Jesus in every human being,' Mother Teresa

replied. 'I say to myself, this is hungry Jesus. This one has gangrene, dysentery or cholera. I must wash him and tend to him.'

I wrote a humble tribute to her for the *New York Times* and put her on the cover of *The Illustrated Weekly*. Till then, she was little known outside Calcutta; after that, more people got to know about her work. She sent me a short note of thanks, which I have in a silver frame in Kasauli. It is among my most valued possessions. It says: 'I am told you do not believe in God. I send you God's blessings.'

I have often thought about those three days I spent with Mother Teresa in Calcutta. We walked through crowded streets, rode in trams to visit her various hospitals, crèches for abandoned children and homes for the dying. I still remember how she tended to a very ill man who was dying. She was with him, looking after him, all the time telling him: 'Bhogoban achhen'—God is there. The way in which Mother Teresa went about looking after and tending to the sick, the dying, the hungry—it was the same as Bhagat Puran Singh.

Some years later, during one of my trips to Calcutta, I requested Mother Teresa to meet me. But she declined, saying that she would not come to my hotel room. It was okay by me, because I respected her. I saw her last when she was in Delhi. She had come here when H.S. Sikand (of Sikand Motors) had gifted a van for her Missionaries of Charity, but this time she did not seem to recognize me. I smiled and greeted her; though she did smile back, she did so in the way you do when you don't really recognize a person.

MUHAMMAD ALI JINNAH

(1876–1948)

Muhammad Ali Jinnah knew my father. In fact, when the Partition was taking place, he had sent word to my father that I stay put there in Lahore and don't shift, and he would appoint me a judge at the Lahore high court. He also attended my wedding reception.

To understand Jinnah's role as an ambassador of Hindu-Muslim unity, a title conferred on him by Sarojini Naidu, one needs to know his background. He was born in Bombay in an Ismaili Khoja family, regarded by orthodox Muslims as 'beliefless'. They were traders and merchants who had more dealings with Parsis and Hindus than with fellow Muslims. In 1897, he converted to the Shia faith. What the conversion entailed is not clear because he never conformed to any religious trends. In 1892, he proceeded to England to study law at Lincoln's Inn. During the four years he was in England, he made it a point to go to the houses of Parliament to listen to debates. He was deeply impressed by the speeches made by Dadabhai Naoroji, the first Indian to be elected to the House of Commons, and John Morley. Both men were liberals. Jinnah accepted them as his role models and liberalism as his political creed. Back home in Bombay, he befriended Sir Pherozeshah Mehta, Gokhale and Badruddin Tyabji. He was determined to pursue the careers of law and politics. He regarded both as gentlemanly professions. Although he married a Parsi girl, Ruttie, many years younger than him, his professional occupations left him little time to discharge his domestic obligations. He was also dour, unsmiling, tense and a chain-smoker. After some years, Ruttie left him with their daughter, Dina (the mother of Nusli Wadia of Bombay Dyeing).

Jinnah was quite clear about the role of Indian politicians. They must never mix religion with politics: one was a private matter, the other public service. Political differences should be settled by debate and not taken to the streets to create mob hysteria. The right to vote should be restricted to the educated tax payer and not be extended to the illiterate and those who do not contribute to the cost of administration. Primary education should be compulsory. What is truly amazing is that he found many takers for his ideas and was acceptable to the Indian National Congress as well as the Muslim League. For some years, he straddled both parties and was accepted by them as their spokesperson. He used his diplomatic skill to reconcile the Muslim League's demands and persuaded the Congress to accept them: separate electorates with weightage for Muslims in states where they were in a minority, and Muslim hegemony in Sindh, Punjab, the NWFP and Bengal, where they formed a majority. He succeeded in bringing about political unity between Hindus and Muslims so that they could jointly pressurize their British rulers to hand over the governance of the country to Indians. In a speech at the Muslim League Conference in Lucknow in 1917, he urged Muslims not to look upon the Hindu majority as a bogey, saying: 'This is a bogey which is put before you by your enemies to frighten you, to scare you away from the cooperation with the Hindus which is essential for the establishment of self-government.' Unlike most other Indian politicians, he was not overwhelmed by English governors and viceroys: he spoke his mind to them without mincing his words. He carried on verbal warfare with Lord Willingdon, Governor of Bombay and then Viceroy of India. In short, he was for a time India's top political leader, till Mahatma Gandhi arrived on the scene. Gandhi not only infused religion into politics but also took politics to the streets through his call for non-cooperation and boycott of government-run institutions, including schools. Jinnah found this distasteful and difficult to digest. Besides these, Gandhi showed a marked preference for Jawaharlal Nehru as the future leader of the country. Gradually, Jinnah was pushed off the centre stage of Indian politics to become more and more a leader of the Muslims.

In any event, Jinnah was elected to the Legislative Council from a Muslim constituency. He was among the Muslim delegates at the Round Table Conference in London. He stayed on in England for a few years and toyed with the idea of fighting elections to the House of Commons. No party was willing to accept him as its candidate. It was not surprising. As *The Manchester Guardian* summed him up: 'The Hindus thought he was a Muslim communalist, the Muslims took him to be pro-Hindu, the princes declared him to be too democratic, the British considered him a rabid extremist—with the result that he was everywhere but nowhere. None wanted him.' Reluctantly, Jinnah returned to Bombay to resume his legal practice and his political career, now as a spokesperson of Muslim interests.

MULK RAJ ANAND

(1905–2004)

Mulk Raj Anand was one of the first three Indian
writers of fiction in English to be published in
England. It is common knowledge that both Mulk's
and R.K. Narayan's first novels were turned down
by a number of English publishers, till they found
sugar daddies whom they could persuade to risk
their money on them. And so, Graham Greene
became a sponsor for R.K. Narayan; Mulk had
the Bloomsbury group, which included T.S. Eliot,
to back him. Only Raja Rao's *Kanthapura* made it
without any sifarish. Needless to say, all the three
were lionized by their countrymen.

Mulk's chief patrons were socialists and communists. They were English men and women who suffered from a sense of guilt over what the British Raj had done to India. Mulk was well aware of what India's rich and powerful had done to the poor and powerless and the humiliations the lower castes had suffered at the hands of the privileged higher castes. These became the theme of many of his novels and short stories. He became the chief spokesperson of the progressive writers who wrote to serve social purposes and did not bother so much about style and turn of phrase. Over time, Mulk's writing became progressively propagandist.

Mulk returned to India after the publication of his first two novels, *Untouchable* and *Coolie*. He was accorded a warm reception by literary groups across the country. The reception he got at Lahore was tepid. A literary circle comprising some judges of the high court, a couple of ICS officers, professors of English literature and lawyers invited him for tea. They had read his novels and felt they could write as well as he did. Mulk sensed the condescending attitude but kept his cool till someone blurted out: 'We can write as well as you, but who will publish us?' Mulk exploded: 'First write, then talk.' Then he walked away in a huff. Many in that circle wrote. Not one was able to break the apartheid of the publishing houses. There were hardly any Indian commercial publishers worth going to. Most of these aspiring writers published their books at their own cost.

Though born in Peshawar, there was nothing Pathan-like about Mulk. He was short, with fuzzy hair, and, like the son of a Punjabi bania, dressed in khadi kurta-pyjamas. He had a strange way of speaking: a lot of lisping and sentences ending in squeaks. But he loved holding forth, and was warm and friendly. He liked living well and enjoyed the company of women. After his marriage to his English wife broke up, he had a Sri Lankan mistress, followed by a Parsi one. He lived in a ground-floor flat on Cuffe Parade, Bombay, facing the sea. I called on him one morning and saw him at work. He was perched on a high chair especially designed for him, with his feet resting below. He was bending over a writing pad.

Mulk had a setback in his later years. He was commissioned by the *Evergreen Review* of New York to do an article on the erotic in Indian art. It was very well-received till the magazine got a legal notice alleging that the article was a copy of one article translated from German to English. Mulk's explanation was naïve beyond belief. Dosu Karaka, editor of the weekly *Current*, who hated the communists' guts, had the news splashed in big headlines: 'Commie Author Caught Plagiarising'. It took some months of retirement to his villa in Lonavala for Mulk to bounce back. But bounce back the man did, and resumed pontificating to audiences across the country. He never took notice of the topic under discussion nor the time set for speakers. He would go on and on about how his father used to beat his mother. He ignored the chairperson's bell and taps on the back. He had his say and never ever repented it. One particular conversation between Mulk and Eliot relays much about the way he could carry on.

'A piece of cake, Mr—?' asked Eliot.

'Anand,' Mulk supplied.

'Oh, like the Scotch Anand.'

'No, it's a derivation from Ananda, one of the names of the Hindu supreme God, meaning bliss. My full name is Mulk Raj Anand, which means "King of the country of happiness"—and I try to look it.'

Friends and admirers of Mulk Raj Anand noticed how Chacha Mulk mellowed with age and how the once acerbic-tongued critic had only the nicest things to say about everyone in the last decade of his life. A great one for dropping names, once upon a time he did not spare anyone. But in his saintlier anecdotage, his compassion turned him into a crashing bore.

PHOOLAN DEVI

(1963-2001)

Sometime in 1982, when I was the editor of the *Hindustan Times*, I got a call from the commissioner of police of Lucknow asking if I could send a reporter to cover the arrest of Phoolan Devi. Instead of sending a reporter I decided to go myself. I was able to reconstruct Phoolan Devi's past from talking to her parents, sisters and one of her lovers, and cross-checking what they told me with the statement she made to the police on 6 January 1979, the first time she was arrested.

It was at Gurh Ka Purua village I that I got a whiff of the romantic life of Phoolan Devi.

Recall that nostalgic film song 'Nadi kinarey mera
gaon'? Everything that the song evokes was there
in Phoolan's story. Young Phoolan—sixteen or
seventeen—left her forty-five-year-old husband, who
aroused her appetite for sex without fulfilling it.
One afternoon, she spied a young mallah bathing
in the river. She watched him for some time and
then asked if she could borrow his cake of soap to
bathe herself. He turned out to be a distant cousin,
Kailash, married but willing to have an extramarital
affair. They got talking. The bathing and soaping
gave Phoolan excuses to show Kailash something
of her form and figure, setting his passions aflame.
They arranged to meet—as most lovers in the region
did—in the arhar fields the next day. They had sex—
surreptitious, hurried and unfulfilling. But it was
enough to make them yearn for more. Kailash was
thoroughly confused; he had a young and attractive
wife, who had borne him four children—and here
was Phoolan, who was giving him something he had
never experienced with his wife. Phoolan agreed to
let him have more on the condition that he married
her. How could he? Meanwhile, the village gossip
mill started grinding: Phoolan Devi had been
discarded by an old husband and was available. The

sarpanch's son approached her. He entertained close friends with the same feast of flesh. Phoolan did not mind, but it was not doing her reputation any good.

When Kailash asked for more, she forced him to marry her. They went to Kanpur, where a lawyer wrote out something on a piece of paper, took fifty rupees from Kailash and told them they were man and wife. They spent two days and nights at the lawyer's house; the days at the movies, the nights making love. Then they returned to Kailash's village, Teonga. Kailash's parents and wife gave Phoolan a sound thrashing and turned her out. She returned crestfallen to her village, Gurh Ka Purua. The sarpanch's son got to hear of her escapade to Kanpur, sent for her and gave her a shoe-beating. At a fair in the neighbouring village, she ran into Kailash's wife, Shanti Devi, and her children. Shanti Devi grabbed Phoolan by the hair, clawed her face and abused her in front of the crowd as a raand, bitch, home-breaker.

By now, all the mallah villages had heard about Phoolan's misadventures. Among them was Bikram Singh, a gangster friend of Kailash. Bikram Singh arrived in Gurh Ka Purua and gave Phoolan the choice of coming with him or having her only brother, Shivnarain Singh—who was only twelve—join his gang. Phoolan went with Bikram to become his mistress. And thus she was launched into her career of crime.

What did Phoolan Devi look like? There were no photographs available. But from my interviews I could construct her image in my mind. Phoolan's younger sister Ramkali was said to resemble her. Ramkali was a sexy and saucy lass, who knew how to strike poses and used her large eyes like sidewinder missiles. She was thick-lipped, big-bosomed and altogether seductive—as they say in Punjabi, well worth a crime. I couldn't take my eyes off her—nor could any of the men in the party accompanying me. In fact, our photographer, Premi, clicked an entire reel on her.

PREM NATH KIRPAL

(1909-2005)

My friendship with Prem Kirpal lasted longer than
any other—over sixty years. Circumstances threw us
together in Lahore, Delhi, London, Paris and back
again in Delhi. We happened to be in England at
the same time, as students: he was in Oxford, I in
London. We heard of each other from common
friends but never met. It was in Lahore, where
I settled down to practise law and he got a job as
a lecturer in Dayal Singh College, that we got to
know each other.

Prem's father, Ishwar Das, was then deputy
registrar, and later registrar, of Punjab University.

They were Sahajdhati Sikhs. Prem's mother came from a family of orthodox Khalsas. Ishwar Das was much influenced by leaders of the Singh Sabha movement, the poet Bhai Veer Singh, Dr Jodh Singh and the Attatiwala family. This was a common link between his family and my wife's parents, who were ardent followers of Bhai Veer Singh. It did not take us long to start visiting each other's homes.

Prem was very conscious of having been a student of Balliol College, Oxford, and always wore his college tie. In his scheme of things, Oxford was the best university in the world, Balliol the best college in Oxford, and he privileged to be the product of the best institution. An anecdote told about him was that when leaving Oxford to catch his boat to return to India, he happened to be having his breakfast in the dining car of the Oxford-London train. Sitting across the table was an Englishman also having breakfast. Over the din and rattle of the train, he asked Prem, 'Would you mind passing me the salt?' Prem promptly held up his college tie and replied, 'Yes, this is a Balliol tie.'

Soon I found out other connections with the Kirpal family. All the sons had been to Government College: Amar Nath, Prem, Pritam and Prakash.

Amar Nath was a lawyer and edited a law journal; his son Bhupinder (Cuckoo) also became a lawyer and, later, judge of the Delhi high court and chief justice of the Gujarat high court. Pritam, who played hockey for the college, retired from the army as a general. Prakash became a draughtsman in the Survey of India in Dehra Dun. There were also three or four sisters, of whom two, Sita and Leela, were then unmarried. Ishwar Das often used to boast of the virility of the Kirpals, when he rued that Prem had not found a wife and kept up the family tradition of fecundity.

Actually, Prem was very eager to find a mate. His first choice was his closest friend Mangat Rai's elder sister. Priobala was then teaching in Kinnaird College. Prem started calling on her. He was not a man of many words—and when it came to women, even less vocal. He was not getting anywhere because in Kinnaird College there were always some women about. At my suggestion, he persuaded Priobala to come out with him for a drive. He did not have a car and could not afford a taxi. So he hired a tonga and the two went around Lawrence Gardens and other beauty spots of Lahore. He was still not getting anywhere. I told him that some women responded to action and that he should simply grab her in his arms and kiss her. He decided to give it a try. The next time he took Priobala for a tonga ride, he told her, 'Prio, you know what Khushwant asked me to do? He said I should take you in my arms and kiss you.' Priobala was incensed. 'He is an absolute rascal. You can tell him that for me,' she added. And that was to remain the pattern of many romances.

After Partition, we found ourselves in Delhi and then London. He was education officer; I was a press attaché. Our boss, Krishna Menon, did not like Prem but liked me to start with. Prem was sent back to the ministry. A couple of years later, I resigned from my job and was back in Delhi. Prem and I resumed our friendship. He was joint secretary and an eligible bachelor.

One afternoon, while sharing the office car with a lady colleague, Prem's hand slipped and fell on her shoulder. The lady promptly responded by giving him a full-blooded kiss on his lips. There was no escape. His father approved of the girl (she was South Indian) and their engagement was announced. What came as a surprise to me was that Prem, now in his forties, knew so little about the female sex. One afternoon, when overcome by passion he tried to bed her, she pleaded illness and begged him to be patient for a few days. That was the first time he had heard of women menstruating. 'Please don't tell anybody I didn't know about this,' he begged me. Of course, I told everyone. The way he broke up with the lady was even more amusing. She fixed the date for their wedding. Prem disappeared from Delhi and sent her a telegram saying he had broken his leg and the marriage would have to be postponed indefinitely. For a few days, he even had his leg put in plaster.

Past experiences did not deter Prem from making passes at young women. And when they responded, he beat a hasty retreat.

What I have said about Prem may make him appear very lightweight. He was not. He became head of the cultural division of UNESCO, member and then chairman of the executive board. Although he knew very little about art or music, either Eastern or Western, he made an excellent chairman and conducted meetings with great skill. His strength lay in gentleness and offending nobody.

Although I made cruel fun of him, Prem remained devoted to my entire family. We travelled all over Europe and Latin America. My accounts of these journeys are peppered with anecdotes about him. Once, in Madrid, I had to bully him to visit the Prado by telling him that it had a richer collection than the Louvre and that his colleagues were bound to ask him about it. He strode through the Prado galleries in fifteen minutes flat. Back in Paris, he told his friends that he thought the Prado was better than the Louvre. They were horrified and told him so. He, in turn, was angry with me for having exaggerated the quality of the Prado.

Another time, still in Madrid, we decided to invite Elizabeth Adiseshiah, who was staying in another hotel with her husband, Malcolm, for dinner as her husband was busy in a conference. Prem went to call up from the hotel telephone in the lobby, which was packed with guests having tea. When he got her on the line, Prem began to shout at the top of his voice: 'Lisbeth, this is Prem. If you are not doing anything, then come and have dinner with us.' Everyone in the lobby stopped talking to listen to the announcement. When he came back, he told me, 'Elizabeth will come for dinner.' I replied, 'I know. So does everyone else in the hotel. Why did you have to shout so loudly?' His reply was classic:

'She is in the other hotel, which is a long distance from here.'

Prem returned to Delhi to become secretary of the ministry of education. He had a strong patron in Dr S. Radhakrishnan, who saw to it that Prem got what he wanted. Prem was not averse to laying on flattery when it was required. 'You are the greatest philosopher in the world today,' he told Radhakrishnan. I could not resist cutting in: 'Sir, he has not read even one of your books.' Prem gracefully acknowledged: 'That is true. I have not read your books, but everyone tells me you are a great philosopher. I accept that.' Prem, who knew little about Radhakrishnan's works, remained his favourite; I, who had read almost everything he had written, was kept at a distance.

After retirement from government service, Prem took on the Delhi Public Schools—perhaps the largest chain of schools in the country. He got me nominated to the board as he needed support against mischief-makers who were forever trying to take over the management. Although DPS kept him busy, he still had a lot of time on his hands. Prem evolved a new pattern of living. He would get up late, then take a long walk in Lodi Gardens.

After lunch, he would take a long siesta before tea. He would be at the India International Centre almost every evening. Back home, he would have yet another bout in bed. By dinnertime, he would be fresher than anyone else. He could not bear to be alone because he did not read—he had the largest unread library in his house. He invited the same people to his dinner parties. And if he could not get anyone, he landed up at my flat with the announcement 'What's happening?' and then stayed on for dinner.

Prem became hard of hearing towards the last years of his life. He also took to painting in the most garish of colours. The walls of his sitting and dining rooms were plastered with his paintings. He also composed poetry at the drop of a hat. He loved to celebrate his birthday, when he kept an open house. Champagne and Scotch flowed. On the centre table, he kept albums. One had pictures of the women he admired or loved; the other was of himself with notables such as Dr Radhakrishnan and the director general of the UNESCO. Beside these albums lay the latest edition of the Balliol College magazine.

It was a sad day for me when he died.

PROTIMA BEDI

(1948–1998)

The two words missing from Protima Bedi's life's lexicon were 'no' and 'regret'. She could never say no to a man who desired her, and grew into a very desirable and animated young woman—whom most men found irresistible. And she did not regret any of the emotional and physical experiences she had.

Protima felt that keeping secrets was like lying, so she told everyone everything, including her husband and the succession of lovers who entered her life. She broke up marriages but remained blissfully unaware of the hurt she caused people. She had to get everything off her ample bosom.

Protima Gauri (as she renamed herself) had a zest for living. She loved men, liquor and drugs. She had an enormous appetite for sex and admitted to enjoying it as many as six times a day. She had a large range of lovers. Protima hated humbugs and hypocrites. She wrote: 'Every woman I know secretly longed to have many lovers but stopped herself for many reasons. I had the capacity to love many at a time and for this had been called shallow and wayward and a good-time girl.'

Protima also had a puckish sense of humour. Once, she arrived in Bombay with an electric vibrator. A very scandalized customs officer refused to let it pass. She gave him a dressing down: 'My husband is out of town most of the time—what do you expect me to do? I am trying to be faithful! Are you encouraging infidelity?' She got away with it.

Death caught Protima unawares. She was killed in a landslide while on a pilgrimage to Badrinath. And on the same day, in Bombay, died Persis Khambatta, India's first beauty queen and the one-time mistress of Protima's husband, Kabir Bedi.

SAHIR LUDHIANVI

(1921–1980)

Sentimental, sensitive, sensuous, generous, but at the same time edgy, quick-tempered, hypersensitive and quarrelsome—Sahir Ludhianvi was all these as well as the best and the most successful of our lyricists. He was also the hardest of drinkers.

Apart from Scotch, what Sahir thirsted for was appreciation. I was surprised at the childish joy with which he celebrated the award of the Padma Shri. And when his fellow Ludhianvis decided to honour him, he travelled all the way to Punjab and back to Bombay by rail (he had a morbid fear of flying) to be acclaimed by his native city.

I had many encounters with Sahir in the homes of common friends in Bombay and spent a few evenings at his house in Juhu, close to where Balraj Sahni lived. If any evening passed without an unpleasant incident, I regarded it as a minor miracle. Sahir was particularly touchy when he found himself in the company of the newly rich who pretended to enjoy shair-o-shairee. There is no dearth of them in Bombay, where the film industry has thrown up as many millionaires as it has spawned versifiers. I recall one evening in particular. A well-meaning Gujarati businessman began praising Sahir, but in the process misquoted one of his lines. Sahir turned on the poor (rich) man with a volume of abuse in a mixture of English and Punjabi-Urdu (he never got rid of his Ludhiana accent) till the other was compelled to leave, and the party was ruined. It transpired that Sahir was not expecting a drink in the house and had been taking slugs of neat Scotch all the way from Juhu to Malabar Hill.

In his own home, Sahir was always very considerate. There was his old-fashioned mother, who spoke nothing but the Malwa dialect of Punjabi, as well as a younger relative and the inevitable bottle of Scotch. I was sure that Sahir's mother disapproved of his heavy drinking. To ingratiate myself in her favour, I asked her, 'Maji, why don't you curb his drinking? Don't you see it's doing him no good?' She replied by asking me: 'Puttar, what can I do when he has friends like you, who come to see him only to drink his whisky?'

SANJAY GANDHI

(1946–1980)

I have been criticized and attacked more often than most people I know. It does not bother me; I ignore it all or laugh it off. The one criticism I have faced that I take seriously is to do with my support for Sanjay Gandhi. In 1975, after Mrs Gandhi declared Emergency in the country, I ran a cover story in the Independence Day issue of *The Illustrated Weekly* on her second son and partner-in-politics, Sanjay. I called it 'The Man Who Gets Things Done'. I have never lived this down, but I stand by the story. I believed that Sanjay was what the country needed at the time—a man of action who would bring discipline in public offices, crack down on smugglers, clean up our cities and, most important, take serious steps to control our explosive population growth. I believed that he was doing all those things and I supported him, perhaps blindly. Outside the moment, it is easy to see the full picture.

I met Sanjay in the mid-1970s, when he was already unpopular among intellectuals and many of my fellow liberals who saw him as an extra-constitutional power and a potential tyrant. When I met him, I found him to be reasonable and courteous. He was the one who had called the meeting. He wanted to talk to me about his Maruti car business and wanted me to write about it. I went with him to the factory site. I was disappointed; it looked like the workshop of a blacksmith, a lohar. He took me around the site in a prototype of the Maruti car, driving fast and talking about how important the project was. I was more impressed by his passion and enthusiasm than by the physical set-up. It was being said in those days that Haryana's chief minister, Bansi Lal, had given Sanjay land for free for his factory. I found these allegations to be false. Sanjay had paid a fair price. I wrote this in my story on Maruti. That was how our association began. We became friends.

Sanjay was good-looking. He had an eye for pretty girls, but the good sense not to get carried away. He was also a teetotaller, but not self-righteous. Always polite, Sanjay sought me out for company and advice. I was flattered. Our friendship was strengthened after his marriage to Maneka, whose family I knew. They made a handsome couple. I was past sixty then and, like many people reaching old age, I enjoyed the attention of young and spirited people.

Since I also had a good equation with Mrs Gandhi in those days, I was dubbed the Gandhis' chamcha, especially when I supported the Emergency. Even now, after all these years, I think the Emergency was necessary, because the opposition had unleashed chaos and nothing in the country functioned. I had no idea then that it could be and would be misused and abused. Sanjay was always extremely courteous to me, so I found it hard to believe stories about his dictatorial ways. When I first got to know him, he really did seem like a committed man who was always true to his word. He had a conscience. And he was a doer, impatient to bring about changes. Maybe that was what made him dictatorial.

A year or so into the Emergency, he became very unpopular because of the forced nasbandi (sterilization) programme, censorship and arbitrary slum demolitions. It was bruited about that he had ordered bulldozers to be run over the jhuggis of innocent people, and that men had been pulled out of buses and cinema halls and forcibly sterilized. Many of these were wild rumours, but it is true that Sanjay and his thuggish friends—they more than he—were beginning to run the country like their fiefdom. Mrs Gandhi had come to depend heavily on her dynamic younger son and had almost handed over the reins of power to him. Nobody could understand the hold he had on her. She both loved and feared him. There is a story that Sanjay once slapped his mother at the dinner table, with outsiders present, and she took it quietly.

What Sanjay did, or was alleged to have done, during the Emergency had given him the image of a monster. He and Maneka came to see me in Bombay shortly after the Congress had been voted out of power, with Mrs Gandhi losing badly in her constituency. When they came to my apartment on

Arthur Bunder Road, there were mobs in the streets baying for Sanjay's blood. I had to drive the couple to the airport at some risk.

I stood by the Gandhi family during their days in the doghouse, when they were being persecuted by the Janata Party government, many of whose leaders the Gandhis had persecuted during the Emergency. My family and friends were very critical of me, and I had to face a great deal of flak. I watched with some satisfaction as Mrs Gandhi and Sanjay fought back and won the elections of 1980. But the happiness was brief. On the morning of 23 June 1980, Sanjay crashed his two-seater plane on the southern ridge in Delhi. Both he and his co-pilot, Captain Saxena, were killed. After his tragic death, it was left to his older brother, Rajiv—with whom he had had very little interaction—to support a shattered Indira Gandhi. There is some truth in the belief that she was never quite herself after Sanjay's death.

I liked Sanjay. But I am certain that if he had lived, this country would not have been a democracy. There would have been order and much faster development, but no democracy. I have been asked if, in that case, I would still have supported him. I don't know. He would probably have got around me. He could be a real charmer. Besides, he was a friend, and he had been good to me. It was because of him that I was nominated to the Rajya Sabha. And it was he who called up K.K. Birla and told him to give me the editor's job at the *Hindustan Times*. He did not need to do that, but he did. He was loyal, and so was I.

SHRADDHA MATA

(191?-1987)

It was during my editorship of the fortnightly
journal *New Delhi* that I first met Shraddha Mata.
I did a long feature article on the tantric sadhvi
who, according to M.O. Matthai, had borne Prime
Minister Nehru an illegitimate child. In the process,
I became quite friendly with her. Whenever I was
in Jaipur, I called on her at her permanent abode,
Hathroi Fort. It was no longer the journalistic
nosiness to probe into her past association with
Pandit Nehru. It was more a spirit of adventure
to explore the world in which she lived and of
which I knew nothing: of round-the-clock prayer,

the tantric rites amongst burning corpses and her
down-to-earth earthiness.

Shraddha Mata was already in her mid-seventies
when I met her, and the most beautiful woman of
her age you would see anywhere. What she must
have looked like in her twenties when she turned
a tantric! She was the stuff dreams are made of:
hair knotted in a bun, ivory complexion, high
cheekbones, full bosom. A tiger skin to cover her
middle and Shiva's trident in her hand. She lived
alone in Hathroi Fort. She spent most of her day
meditating in a tiny windowless cell dug in the
ramparts of the fort. The lookout tower had been
converted into a shrine to the Goddess Durga; there,
she kept vigil till the early hours, performing tantric
rituals and weird ceremonials while the world slept.
The fortress was infested with snakes and scorpions.
Also mice and mosquitoes. She refused to let anyone
kill them—taking life, according to her, was God's
prerogative. Her closest companions were a pack of
friendly dogs, all jet-black.

During the day, Shraddha Mata sometimes
received visitors seated on her takht posh, crown
dais, draped in saffron robes; the visitors would
have to squat uncomfortably on the bare floor, her

dogs sprawled between her and them. On one visit, she said to me: 'Tell people of Mahashakti of the third eye, through which Truth is revealed. Warn the people against pursuing materialism; it will spell the ruin of the world.' She talked of the Kendra Bindu and the teachings of the saints. She turned to the conjunction of the planets and their effect on humans. 'If only Sanjay had come to see me as I had asked him to do, I would have given him a jap that would have saved his life. I met Sanjay only once, when he was holidaying with his family in Kashmir. He was then a little boy. I could see in his eyes that he was going to be tejasvi [radiant personality]. Sanjay's son, Varun, is destined to be the reviver of Hinduism. Once I told Panditji that he was destroying the sacred threads of the Hindus, his grandson would put them back.'

On another occasion, I touched her feet and asked about her health. She told me about her diabetes. 'It was the water in England that brought it on,' she said. 'I was there to inaugurate a Shakti temple in Sussex. They put me on insulin.' The diabetes had affected her vision. At times, it brought a high fever. 'One day, it shot up to 105,' she said. 'Medicines did not help. I brought it down to normal by chanting the right mantra.' She read disbelief in my eyes and decided to cut me to size: 'The first time you came to see me at Nigambodh Ghat, I called you an "ulloo ka pattha". You put it down in your column in English as "son of an owl".' She laughed at her own joke.

That was the tenor of all our meetings.

TIKKA KHAN

(1915–2002)

The Bangladesh war had just ended, and I was as eager to be the first Indian journalist to interview General Tikka Khan as he was determined to have nothing to do with any Indian. He was angry that he had been dubbed by the Indian press as the 'Butcher of Bengal' and was smarting under the ignominious defeat inflicted by the Indian Army on Pakistan. He did not acknowledge my letter asking for an interview; it was my friend Manzur Qadir who interceded on my behalf and persuaded him to talk to me as 'a friend of Pakistan'.

General Tikka Khan received me courteously in his bungalow. He was a short, stocky man with a dour expression—he looked more like a bank clerk than a soldier. With him was his orderly, a huge man in a Pathan-style skull cap with a stiffly-starched turban. As I looked around, I noticed the paraphernalia usual in the homes of army top brass—regimental insignias, trophies and photographs in silver frames. On the mantelpiece and the walls were quotations from the Koran, including one that I was able to decipher. I kept it to myself as I felt it might come in handy in my dialogue with the general.

Tikka Khan was a bitter man. He maintained that stories published in the Indian and foreign press, of mass killings and gang rapes committed by Pakistanis, were untrue. 'We are a God-fearing people, my soldiers were a disciplined body of men. They didn't go about shooting innocent Bengalis and molesting their women. It is you Indians who spread these lies and had British newspapers publish these calumnies against us,' he said, looking directly into my eyes.

I made a mild protest. I told him that I had visited Bangladesh soon after the war and heard stories of atrocities committed by Pakistani troops and officers from the mouths of Bangladeshi Muslims. 'They could not all be lies,' I said. 'And I saw the enormous anger against Pakistanis. But for the Indian troops to protect them, Pakistani prisoners of war would have been lynched by Bangladeshi mobs.'

'There might have been a few incidents,' the general finally conceded. 'There are some black sheep in every herd. And you know how prone Bengalis are to exaggerating everything!' He then quoted an Urdu couplet:

Shauq-e-tool-o-peych iss zulmat qade mein hai
    agar
Bangaali ke baat sun aur Bangaalan ke baal
    dekh

If you like to add length to a story, put a twist
    in its tail
Hear a Bengali talk (endlessly) and gaze upon
    his woman's long hair

I found this very amusing and put it down in my notebook, fodder to tease my Bengali friends with.

I asked the general why Pakistan had put up such a miserable performance on the field of battle.

'It was not a fair fight,' he replied. 'First, you cut off air contact between West and East Pakistan. Then your men infiltrated deep inside East Pakistan, long before we were compelled to declare war. All these stories of the Mukti Bahini were propaganda. The Mukti Bahini were Indian soldiers trained for guerrilla warfare; there were very few Bengalis in it to start with. You armed them, your officers led and directed them. Our troops had to face the enemy in front as well as in their rear.'

The orderly volunteered his opinion: 'Awaam humare khilaaf ho gaya tha'—the people had turned against us.

The general did not approve of his orderly expressing an opinion and raised his hands to silence him. But I cashed in on the pronouncement. 'That is exactly what I have been saying. What can an army do if the entire populace of a country rises against it?'

'It was Indian propaganda,' maintained the general.

I did not have very much more to ask him. I pointed to the quotation from the Koran on the mantelpiece and, feigning innocence, asked, 'What does it mean?'

The general read it out loudly: 'Nasr min Allah Fateh-un qareeb. It means: Allah grants victory to those whose cause is just.'

'General Sahib, Allah in His wisdom granted us victory because our cause was just.'

For the first time during the interview, the General smiled. 'Sardar Sahib, I suspect you knew what the quotation meant.'

I admitted I did and took my leave.

In the years that followed my interview with him, General Tikka Khan was imprisoned several times as the political climes of Pakistan changed. After Zulfiqar Ali Bhutto's execution in 1979, he emerged as one of the leaders of the Pakistan People's Party and rose to the coveted position of Governor of Punjab during Benazir Bhutto's tenure as prime minister and finally retired from politics in 1990. Adamant about his beliefs and the justness of his cause, the Butcher of Balochistan and Bengal spent the last years of his life in illness and died in 2002.

VIDIADHAR SURAJPRASAD NAIPAUL

(1932-)

When I got the news of V.S. Naipaul being awarded the Nobel Prize for literature, I was delighted and felt I had been vindicated. I was delighted because I had known him as a friend for decades; I felt vindicated because every time I wrote about him I said he deserved the Nobel Prize as he was a much better writer than many other Nobel laureates. He handled the English language with greater finesse than any other contemporary writer and his range of interests were wider: humour, history, travelogue, religion, clash of civilizations, personal profiles, and so on.

I had met Naipaul's first wife, who was English, and got on famously with his charming, vivacious present wife, Nadira, who is a Pakistani Punjabi. I met his late brother, Shiva, and saw quite a lot of his mother when she visited Delhi. Whether it was in Delhi or in Bombay, throwing a party for Vidia was a must. I took him with me wherever I went. He liked being entertained and meeting new people. He never returned the hospitality. That did not matter as everyone felt privileged to have him in their house and to be able to drop his name.

I had the opportunity of interviewing Naipual with Bhaichand Patel on 8 May 2000. He didn't relish being interviewed. Bhaichand Patel and I were very exercised over the destruction of the Babri Masjid and heckled him for what was widely believed to be the Sangh Parivar's view of the act of vandalism. Naipaul stood his ground. He was an outside observer, not concerned with the rights and wrongs of destroying a mosque. The phrase he used was: 'It was a balancing of history'. I interpreted this to imply that deep in the Hindu psyche was the resentment that Muslin invaders had destroyed hundreds of their temples, so what was so devilish about destroying a dilapidated old mosque?

Naipaul's *Among the Believers: An Islamic Journey* caused a lot of uneasiness amongst Muslims. Even Salman Rushdie accused him of harbouring anti-Muslim feelings. What Naipaul wrote cannot be faulted. He observed that people who accepted Islam wrote off their pre-Islamic past. This phenomenon can be verified in Muslim countries today. In Egypt, the Pharaonic period, which produced the pyramids, the Sphinx and many beautiful temples, is only of historic interest, bringing in tourists and foreign exchange. It is the same in Pakistan. They have consigned their Hindu and Buddhist past to archives, museums and history books. Even the period of Sikh dominance is brushed aside as of little consequence. The destruction of the Buddhas in Bamiyan is a recent example of erasing a pre-Islamic past. This can be seen in all Muslim nations, including the most Westernized ones like Turkey, Morocco and Tunisia. Naipaul did not invent this fact of history; he only exposed it.

Known for being aggressive, Naipaul mellowed a great deal after marrying the highly animated and attractive Nadira. He was not as gruff and edgy as he was, and for good reason started writing about sex with remarkable candour and erotic artistry. Of course, he continues to raise the hackles of people with his comments, especially about other writers. But analysing a litterateur's criticism of literature is the matter for another book.

THE ZAKARIAS

FATMA AND RAFIQ

When I took over as editor of *The Illustrated Weekly* in Bombay, the last of the staff to be interviewed by me was 'Aunty Wendy'. This happened to be Fatma, wife of Rafiq Zakaria, then a senior minister in the Maharashtra government. She was not on the payrolls of *The Weekly* but brought in her contribution and proofread it once a week. She had been told that I meant to abolish 'Aunty Wendy', and came armed with a letter stating that she would not be writing for the journal any longer. I read it and tore it up. 'I am dismissing "Aunty Wendy", not you,' I said. 'If you wish to continue your association with *The Weekly*, we can think of other things that you could do.' She nodded her head, then invited me to her home for dinner to meet her husband and children.

The Zakarias took me by storm. They were a tempestuous family, where shouting at each other was followed by periods of comparative calm. Rafiq had an uncontrollable temper; one never knew when he would flare up. Fatma was more contained but determined to get what she wanted by persistent nagging. They entertained a great deal but only invited people who could further Rafiq's career. He was brought into politics by Morarji Desai, once chief minister of Maharashtra; for years, his portrait had the place of honour in the Zakaria sitting room. When Morarji Desai went out of favour, his portrait was removed and replaced by that of Yashwant Rao Chavan, the then chief minister of Maharashtra.

Fatma helped Rafiq in achieving his political ambitions. She made his engagements, confirmed them every morning and kept his files in order. He wanted to distinguish himself from his colleagues by appearing to be a man of letters. Here too his wife helped him in collecting material and editing what he wrote. After a book on Indian Islam, he and his wife wrote a fictional biography of Razia Sultana. I had given it an unfavourable review; they thought I had praised it. For reasons known only to him, Rafiq suspected me of being prejudiced against Muslims: my dispensing with 'Aunty Wendy', he thought, was meant to dispense with the part-time services of a Muslim.

At my first evening with the Zakarias, we took measure of each other. They served me Scotch; Rafiq kept up the pretence that being a member of the Congress party he did not touch liquor. I was told that I wasn't to tell anyone that I was served whisky in their home. The three boys, Mansoor (from Rafiq's first wife), Arshad and Fareed, gaped at me in disbelief; they had been brought up on stereotyped notions about Sikhs, that they hated Muslims and went berserk at noon, etc. Fatma's mother, a big, portly woman who was staying with them, had warned them against using taxis driven by Sikhs. She couldn't quite make out what I was doing in their home and to her last day referred to me as chhapeywala—the fellow from the printers. Other members of the household included a Goan Man Friday called Pascal Lobo; a wafer-thin Maharashtrian maidservant, with protruding teeth, called Vasanthi; and a cook I called 'The Assassin' because he looked as if he could poison in my food. I was able to come to terms with all of them save the cook and the dog. The cook never exchanged a word with me; the dog bared its fangs at me whenever I came or left.

Rafiq began his bulldozing tactics early on. Why didn't I give his wife a permanent job on the staff? He could speak to the chairman of the company, retired Justice K.T Desai, and the general manager, Tarneja, but the initiative had to come from me. I had no idea how good or bad a worker Fatma could prove to be, but I could not resist the pressure put on me. I thought I might try her out as a subeditor and see how she acquitted herself. But Rafiq dictated the proposal that I sent to the management—Fatma was to be one of the three assistant editors. Rafiq spoke to Desai and Tarneja. The proposal was promptly accepted.

Within a few days, Fatma was installed as assistant editor and quietly assumed the powers of my senior-most aide. No one could see me without being cleared by her; all telephone calls to me were first received by her. Even my social life came to be regulated by her. At least twice a week, I had dinner with her and Rafiq; on other days, if I had not been invited out, food was sent to my apartment. Fatma proved to be an extremely possessive woman who could not tolerate my making friends with other women or men she did not approve of. There was, however, a very positive side to her character. Although she did not and could not write, she organized the commissioning and publishing of articles. She was an excellent sub and unsparing in her endeavour to see *The Weekly* come up. Her dedication to her job and to me was complete. Without her, I could not have run the journal.

ZIAUR RAHMAN

(1936–1981)

I had the privilege of meeting both Sheikh Mujibur
Rahman and President Ziaur Rahman many
times. They were as unlike as any two persons I
have known could be; apart from being Bengali
Muslims, they had nothing in common. Mujib
was above average in height for a Bengali, flabby
and sloppily dressed. Zia was short, slim and made
as if of whipcord. 'His punch can make a man
senseless,' his bodyguard had once told me. Mujib
was warm-hearted, outgoing and garrulous, Zia was
distant, reserved and a man of few words. Mujib's
office was like an oriental durbar of the Mughal

times: dozens of people squatting on the carpets, sprawling on the sofa and chairs, standing along the walls. Telephones rang continuously; he answered them while carrying on conversation with whoever happened to get his attention and signed papers placed on the table. It was chaotic. Zia's office was as cold as he. In the waiting room, his secretaries and security staff discreetly engaged you in polite conversation while their eyes searched your person for concealed weapons. He received his visitors one at a time and stuck to a stopwatch schedule. No one dared to walk into his room unannounced, no telephones buzzed. Your questions froze in the air; his measured answers did not unfreeze them. Mujib insisted on embracing you and calling you an old friend on your second meeting. Zia gave you a stiff shake of his cold hand and a faint smile of recognition. Mujib spoke of himself in the third person, 'Banglabandhu says', and expected you to address him likewise. Zia never opened up, nor let anyone become too familiar with him. He was always 'Mister', 'President', 'Sir'.

I first met Ziaur Rahman after he had been in office for two years. I had my reservations about military dictators and a distinct distaste for one who instead of punishing the assassins of Mujib had rewarded them with diplomatic assignments. Nevertheless, the little I saw of the Dacca environs in the week I spent in Bangladesh was most impressive. The city which had been in shambles a few years earlier had become orderly, with signs of prosperity burgeoning from its shopping centres and marketplaces. They had harvested a bumper crop of rice and the countryside looked greener, cleaner and more prosperous than I had ever seen it. I told Zia this; he looked very pleased and extended my interview. My last question to him was about the anti-India feeling growing in his country. Many walls had slogans painted on them: 'Indian dogs, get out', 'Hands off Bangladesh'. I asked Zia if he could give any instances of Indian interference in his country's affairs. All that he could mention was the Indian government giving asylum to Tiger Siddiqi and Sheikh Mujibur Rahman's family. I countered this by asking him why no one had been arrested or punished for the Banglabandhu's murder. He made no comment but looked at his watch impatiently. I knew the interview was over.

I was Zia's last visitor that evening. He was walking down the corridor a few yards ahead of me, between two enormous bodyguards. It was then that I noticed how short he was—a little over five feet. He wore high-heeled shoes.

ACKNOWLEDGEMENTS

I thank Humra Quraishi, Ravi Singh and Pradipta Sarkar for helping me put this book together.

Most of my books and columns would not have been possible without Lachman Das, my secretary for fifty years. I am grateful to him.

ABOUT THE AUTHOR

Born in Punjab's Hadali village (now in Pakistan) in 1915, KHUSHWANT SINGH is one of India's best known and most widely read authors and columnists. He was founder-editor of *Yojana*, and editor of *The Illustrated Weekly of India*, *National Herald* and the *Hindustan Times*. His first book, *The Mark of Vishnu and Other Stories*, was published in 1950, and he has published several acclaimed and best-selling books of fiction and non-fiction in the six decades since. Among these are the novels *Train to Pakistan*, *I Shall Not Hear the Nightingale*, *Delhi* and *The Company of Women*; his autobiography, *Truth, Love and a Little Malice*; the two-volume *A History of the Sikhs*; a collection of prayers and precepts, *The Freethinker's Prayer Book*; and the forthcoming *Consolations and Lamentations*. He has also translated the work of major Punjabi and Urdu poets and writers, as well as *The Japji and the Rehras: The Morning and Evening Prayers of the Sikhs*.

Khushwant Singh was a member of the Rajya Sabha from 1980 to 1986. He was awarded the Padma Bhushan in 1974; he returned the award in 1984 to protest the siege of the Golden Temple by the Indian Army. In 2007, he was awarded India's second highest civilian honour, the Padma Vibhushan. He was also honoured by the Government of Punjab with the Punjab Rattan Award in 2006.